Text by Trevor Hall
Designed by Philip Clucas MSIAD
Produced by Ted Smart and David Gibbon

Featuring the photography of David Levenson and Neil Sutherland

# A YEAR IN THE LIFE
## OF THE
# ROYAL
# FAMILY

## CRESCENT BOOKS
### New York

# Queen Elizabeth

If, like most of her immediate predecessors, the Queen keeps a regular journal, and is in the habit of recalling the events of each year or other periods of time by a few words summarising their overall impact on her, it will be interesting to know how she has condensed

her impressions of the months between June 1981 and August 1982, the period covered by this book. Its events do not easily telescope into a stereotype of disaster, serenity or even featureless mediocrity. They have come thick and fast, sometimes almost tumbling over each other in their urgency, and all with such variations of character that it is impossible to state that the year has been essentially a good one or a bad one.

Spectacular trooping. The ceremony on 12th June was darkened by the incident in which shots were fired at the Queen. A momentary pallor on the Queen's face betrayed her alarm, but the show went on. For Lady Diana it was a balcony début.

The elements of personal happiness within her family are obvious – a spectacular royal wedding which sent her affable and popular son and heir into married life with a young lady who has effortlessly caught the imagination of the world; the birth, safe and sound, of the infant who, God willing, will secure the succession to the Throne to the second generation; the safe return of her second son from the horrors of a perilous war in the South Atlantic; the thirtieth anniversary of her own accession, which she spent in personal seclusion, though amid official plaudits and public praise and congratulation. But there were alarms and disappointments too – a dramatic incident at the Trooping, demonstrations in Australia and New Zealand, a succession of intruders at Buckingham Palace, a spell of difficult relationships with the Press, the circumstances in which the Queen's senior police officer resigned his post, and the prospect, for the umpteenth time, of a dip into private funds to subsidise Civil List payments which only just kept pace with the rate of inflation.

In retrospect, the overwhelming preoccupation of the year has been with the Queen's security, and no event prompted the anxieties more effectively than the incident in the Mall on 12th June 1981 when

Heirs and graces at Ascot. Lady Diana kept a low fashion profile: purple and white on 15th June, plain peach on 16th, vivid red on 17th and an Edwardian touch in blue and white on 18th. Prince Charles spent two of the days in America.

17-year-old Timothy Marcus Sarjeant fired a series of blank shots at the Queen as she passed by on her way to the Trooping the Colour ceremony on Horse Guards Parade. The worst he did was to alarm the Queen who managed to regain sufficient control of her mount to avoid her bolting, and he was easily set upon by four or five fellow spectators, a couple of Guardsmen and hordes of police who came streaming across the road. He was arrested and taken away for questioning which revealed, as details of his trial in September showed, that he had been obsessed by the idea of assassination as a means of achieving fame, and that had he not been thwarted by his inability to obtain ammunition he would very probably have accomplished his objective. He was sentenced to five years in prison and the Court of Appeal turned down his appeal the following February.

In an odd sort of way everything about the attack seemed unbelievable, involving as it did the Sovereign's personal safety which, because it had hitherto been so effectively protected, seemed almost inviolable. But events were soon to show that all was not well in the Royal Household. In September two footmen were sent for trial on charges of stealing dynamite and equipment from a mine in Gloucestershire, and it was revealed that some of their haul had been stored at Buckingham Palace. The following June former employees

The wedding of the Prince of Wales on 29th July was monumental – visually, musically and emotionally. Everyone denied remembering anything like it before. It all went too perfectly, and the only unplanned incident was the kiss that almost became an historic event.

at the Palace gave the Press details of their activities and those of their invited friends, which indicated that security there was virtually non-existent, and the same month a clerk at the Palace was fined £50 for a drug offence. But the more sinister developments involved those with no connections with the Palace and the period from June to September 1981 was thick with incidents involving intruders. In

June three German tourists easily entered the Palace garden, innocently believing it to be part of Hyde Park; in August a man was found in the grounds, claiming that he was looking for Princess Anne; in September Derek Wapshott was committed for trial for carrying an offensive weapon in the vicinity of the Palace; and the same month a young woman was found looking for Prince Charles in the garden of Highgrove House. New security measures were drawn up between the Queen's police officer, Commander Michael Trestrail, and Scotland Yard, and for a while the concern appeared to die down.

But early the following summer all that changed. On 12th July it was revealed that three days earlier a man had, incredibly, gained

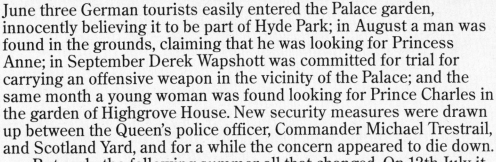

access to Buckingham Palace, walked along its corridors and entered the Queen's bedroom. He sat on the edge of her bed, talked with her – somewhat bitterly – about his problems, drank her wine and asked her for cigarettes. This last request gave the Queen the opportunity, which she took, of ringing for help and the intruder, Michael Fagan, was eventually removed and taken into police custody for questioning. But when the news was released, everyone wanted to know how the lapses in security could have arisen. MP's bombarded the Home Secretary with questions he could not answer until further enquiries were made, and the Press seethed with righteous indignation about the dangers to the Queen.

In the overwhelming furore Commander Trestrail offered the Queen his resignation, which she refused to accept. A week later she changed her mind in the light of one of the most wretched scandals

The honeymoon's foreign leg began with a flight from Eastleigh Airport on 1st August, and the embarkation from Gibraltar amid disgruntled noises from the Spaniards. There was less controversy back at Balmoral: the Prince and his lady rendezvous'd with the world's Press on 19th August.

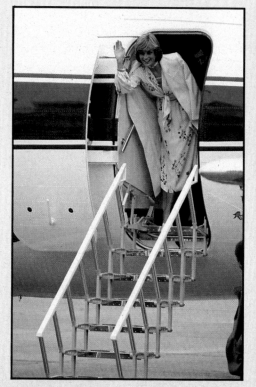

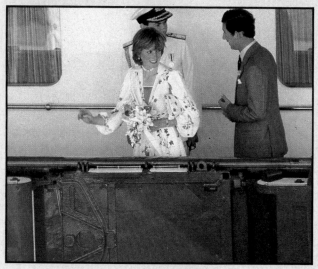

she has ever been concerned to investigate. Commander Trestrail himself confessed the truth of revelations, which had been made to the Press, that he had for some years been seeing a male prostitute and acknowledged that, in theory at least, his liaison could have had implications which might affect the Queen's security. Amid another barrage of questions in the House of Commons, centring around the vetting procedures adopted in the case of officials as close to the Queen as he had been, the unfortunate Commander resigned and disappeared into obscurity, his nine years of loyal and dedicated service almost unacknowledged in the continuing debate.

It may take some strength of will and nerve to continue one's official duties in the full glare of publicity, particularly when the publicity is not all favourable, but the Queen's frequent appearances during one of the busiest months in her calendar amazed even the most cynical observers. At a time when she may herself have wanted to crawl into a hole and forget the world outside, she put everything behind her as she concerned herself with the events she was to attend and the people she was to meet. It was the height of the royal garden party season and the Queen was her usual calm and collected self as she entertained over twenty thousand guests in the grounds of Buckingham Palace that month. The remainder of her heavy schedule of engagements was accomplished in the same serene manner – broken only by the operation she underwent for the removal of a wisdom tooth on 17th July. That operation was performed at the King Edward VII Hospital for Officers, and it was the first time the Queen had ever been to a hospital for medical treatment. Following the Princess of Wales' confinement in hospital only a month earlier, it seemed that royal traditions were being broken thick and fast.

The problems and difficulties of those days in July clouded a year which for the most part had been a happy and successful one.

The Queen's eighth visit to Australia began on 26th September. Despite an early bomb scare at Melbourne, average-sized crowds showed persistent support for their Queen (this page). The usual mix of official greeting and spontaneous gifts, as in Hobart (opposite), was found everywhere. Prime Minister Malcolm Fraser frequently accompanied the Queen (opposite, top right).

The Queen had paid her eighth visit to Australia in September, and her sixth to New Zealand in October. She was absent from London for a month and came home to great praise for maintaining Britain's, and the monarchy's, reputation abroad. The Australians and New Zealanders were less enthusiastic than the Sri Lankans, being more accustomed to seeing the Queen and more inclined to voice their dissention with either her visit or Britain's domestic or foreign policies. The Queen and Prince Philip thus found themselves facing several demonstrations sympathising with the prisoners in Northern Ireland's H-Blocks, almost a dozen of whom had starved to death in a

series of hunger strikes in protest against their lack of political status. In Melbourne there was a bomb scare on the Queen's first full day, and at Dunedin and Wellington in New Zealand mysterious explosions kept the security forces on their toes. Much of the Queen's time in Australia was spent meeting the Prime Ministers of the forty or more Commonwealth countries who had assembled in

Melbourne for the Commonwealth Heads of Government meeting. As always, potential disagreement was in the air and the Queen's neutral presence helped to put things into perspective. One Australian newspaper talked of her influence in the affectionate headline: "55-year-old Grandmother Cools The Family Squabbles."

In Sri Lanka, despite a state of emergency, arising out of economic policies, there was no hint of opposition, or even indifference, to the Royal visit. As the first since the great Commonwealth tour of 1953/54, it was the talking point of the whole country for months beforehand and the arrangements were suitably grand. A wonderfully ceremonial welcome at Colombo airport set the scene: the Queen attended three magnificent banquets, was present at a delightful ceremony celebrating the fiftieth anniversary of the Sri Lankan universal vote, saw the seat of the Buddhist faith in Sri Lanka – the sacred Bo tree and its shrine at Anuradhapura – and

Business with pleasure. In Perth, the Queen's duties were formal in concept (opposite and bottom pictures), but the studious looks at Caulfield Racecourse (right) revealed real interest.

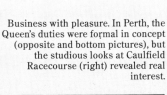

witnessed such extremes of the national way of life as the glittering *perahera,* a torchlight procession of elephants, dancers, jugglers, choirs and bands, staged in her honour at Kandy, and the massive £100 million Victoria Dam project at Pogolla. So interested was she in the latter that she asked for photographs and a progress report to be sent to Buckingham Palace every six months. The Queen made a point of expressing her appreciation of the warmth of her reception throughout her visit. Huge crowds turned out at every possible juncture to catch even the merest glimpse of her, and were happy to

wait long hours, even in the worst downpours that the monsoons could contrive, to cheer her on her long, twisting and bumpy car ride from Anuradhapura to Kandy. It was a brilliant tour, four days of ceremony, colour and popular spontaneity with an appeal that crossed every religious and social barrier.

The Queen and Prince Philip were scheduled to pay a State Visit

The Queen in relaxed spirits at the Perth Agricultural Show at Claremont on 7th October (below), and again on the 10th, when she met ethnic communities in Adelaide (right) and saw the South Australian Derby at Morphettville (bottom right).

to Sweden in June as guests of their cousin King Carl XVI Gustav, but Queen Silvia announced in December that she was expecting her third child – Princess Madeleine, born on 10th June – and the visit was postponed. Some compensation may have been derived from the comparatively impromptu visit which the Queen and Prince Philip made to Ottawa in mid-April, to attend a ceremony at which Canada's last remnant of legislative dependence on Britain was to be excised. After many decades of wrangling between various parties in Canada, the method by which the old Dominion should acquire the right to effect changes to her own constitution had been agreed upon, and the

Queen presided over the formal procedures. She spent three full days in Canada – accompanied on two of them by Prince Philip – attending Government receptions, touring the Parliament Buildings and opening extensions to them, but the highlight was the signing of the Proclamation giving effect to the new law. It was done in grand style, *al fresco* and under the threat of a thunderstorm which finally broke just as the Queen began to speak, but with a superb ceremonial which included the use of bright red thrones, a century-old landau and the full panoply of the Canadian Mounties and Armed Forces. In her speech the Queen regretted the absence of any representation from separatist Quebec, whose sympathisers and supporters were even then demonstrating in local parks against the Queen's visit and the transfer of constitutional power to an English-

A gusty welcome in New Zealand on 12th October (opposite and below) was followed by a bright and warm walkabout in Christchurch (left) the next day.

speaking majority. But she saw her duty as clear – and to prove it she had missed her annual equestrian treat, four days at the Badminton Horse Trials.

As Head of State the Queen also entertained foreign visitors to Britain during the year. The only State Visit occurred in March when the Sultan of Oman repaid a visit made by the Queen to his country in 1979. There was crucial importance in the visit by one of Britain's most reliable friends in the Arabian peninsula, and before the Sultan had left, one Government order for British tanks, two massive industrial orders and an assurance that oil would continue to flow through the Straits of Hormuz were secured. The Queen who, with the Duke, is a great personal friend of the Sultan, promised that "we shall never lose faith with Oman."

In May the Queen received the Pope in a forty-minute audience – more of a courtesy visit during an essentially pastoral tour of the country than the controversies over his coming gave credit for – and a week later Windsor Castle was the setting for a splendid welcome for President and Mrs Reagan, in Britain for a three-day official visit.

Cheerful, but slow, progress in Dunedin (bottom pictures). The Queen is shown her own engagement photograph by one loyalist in the crowd (opposite). Fashion spotters noted the change of jewellery from the last time the Queen wore the same outfit – in Tasmania ten days earlier (below and right).

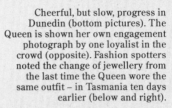

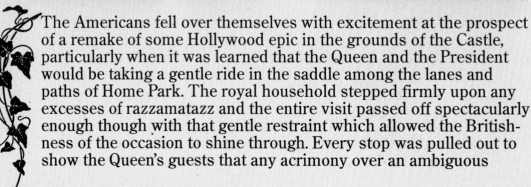

The Americans fell over themselves with excitement at the prospect of a remake of some Hollywood epic in the grounds of the Castle, particularly when it was learned that the Queen and the President would be taking a gentle ride in the saddle among the lanes and paths of Home Park. The royal household stepped firmly upon any excesses of razzamatazz and the entire visit passed off spectacularly enough though with that gentle restraint which allowed the British-ness of the occasion to shine through. Every stop was pulled out to show the Queen's guests that any acrimony over an ambiguous

American stance in the early days of the Falklands crisis was forgiven and, with the superlative State banquet at Windsor on the Reagans' last night, they could have been left in no doubt at all about Britain's attitude.

The glitter and expansiveness of the Windsor banquet brought home to many who may not have realised it before, the colossal organisation and expense of entertaining on the grand scale, and

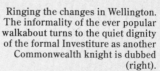

Ringing the changes in Wellington. The informality of the ever popular walkabout turns to the quiet dignity of the formal Investiture as another Commonwealth knight is dubbed (right).

reinforced the absolute necessity of maintaining the Civil List on an economically viable basis. In recent years the size of the annual increase in what is wrongly and mischievously called the Queen's pay has been slightly above the rate of inflation, and has attracted criticism as a result. But in the two years to December 1981 the Queen has had to fund shortfalls in Civil List allowances by payments totalling almost £200,000 from her private resources and

she was probably hoping for an increase in 1982 which would put an end to this necessity. If so she was disappointed, because in March the Chancellor of the Exchequer announced an increase averaging just above 8%. Within three weeks it was revealed by Buckingham Palace that reductions in staff would be made during the year in order to save cash, with personnel doubling up on existing duties,

Maori Queen. Elizabeth II, wearing an unlikely combination of Western straw hat and kiwi feathers, and carrying an umbrella, watched the traditional Polynesian welcome at Auckland on 17th October (right and below). A visit to Hamilton (opposite) brought the New Zealand visit close to its conclusion.

work being contracted out and additional machinery being purchased to dispense with the need to retain staff, whose salaries increased by approximately 6% during the year.

The delicate nature of the Queen's finances is never better exemplified than during the whirlwind of public comment that invariably follows a Civil List increase, though 1982 proved something of an exception. In the absence of a specific opportunity to criticise on this occasion, those MP's who can habitually spare a

grumble or two for the Royal Family found other outlets for their feelings. A periodic target of complaint is the Royal Yacht *Britannia,* reckoned to cost as much as £2.7 million annually to run. Her main uses during the year were for the Prince and Princess of Wales' honeymoon, the Queen and Prince Philip's visit to Australasia, the Queen Mother's tour of the Cinque Ports and during the fortieth anniversary celebrations of the St Nazaire Society in France. When the Falklands crisis erupted, Labour MP Mr Denis Canavan suggested that the *Britannia* should be used as a troopship and requisitioned for Government service like many other luxury craft. He was not convinced by the argument for not doing so – evidently the *Britannia* uses a heavier grade fuel that would give refuelling problems – and his colleague Mr Bob Cryer complained that when, a few years previously, she had been given an expensive refit, it was justified to Parliament partly on the grounds that she could be used

Whilst at Hamilton on 19th October, the Queen visited Middlepark Stud to see her own New Zealand-sired foal, Annie, and some of the best Jersey cows.

in an emergency. An alternative suggestion that the *Britannia* should be used as a replacement for the requisitioned *SS Uganda,* so that a large party of schoolchildren whose holiday in her was interrupted would not lose out, was similarly not taken up.

During the course of the year the deaths occurred of no fewer than seven servants or former servants of the Queen and Prince Philip. Perhaps the most distinguished of them was Sir Alan Lascelles, who died in August 1981 at the age of 94. He had been Private Secretary to Edward Prince of Wales as long ago as 1920, and ultimately became Private Secretary to King George VI and the

The first royal visit to Sri Lanka since 1954 was all smiles. Crowds of villagers waiting for hours laughed the rain off (this page). The Queen took the ceremonies to mark the fiftieth anniversary of the Sri Lankan franchise more seriously (opposite). With her were the Duke and President Jayewardine.

present Queen until 1953. His active dislike of King Edward VIII's somewhat superficial ways and the loyalty and efficiency with which he served his successors make him an indispensible contributor, when the time is appropriate, to the written history of the monarchy. His death was followed in October by that of Sir Alec Coryton, who taught King George VI (then Prince Albert) to fly, in 1919. By the middle of 1982 four members of the Queen's medical staff had also died. A former honorary Physician to the Queen, Major-General Ernest Hood, committed suicide after a prolonged bout of depression.

Dr Marjorie Blackie, the Queen's Physician since 1969, and champion of the homeopathic system of treatment which the Queen has adopted, died in August 1981. And in May 1982, a former Physician to

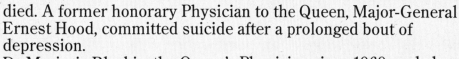

the Queen in Scotland, Sir Ian Hill, and the well-known Sir Ronald Bodley Scott, whose twenty-four year royal service ended in 1973, died – Sir Ronald being fatally injured in a car crash in Italy.

But perhaps the most deeply felt death of 1982 was that of Lord Rupert Nevill who died in July, after a long illness, at the age of only 59. He came into Prince Philip's service in 1970 as his treasurer, and graduated to the trusted post of Private Secretary, coping admirably with the constant stream of correspondence connected with the Duke's enormously busy and varied public life.

# Prince Philip

And life for Prince Philip became no less busy during the year. He completed 1981 with over three hundred engagements at home and a tally of eleven trips abroad – and that was before the consequences of his becoming President of World Wildlife Fund International in May had properly set in. That particular appointment took him in February and March 1982 on an eleven-nation tour of WWF projects as a first step in familiarising himself

Unpronounceable names but unforgettable places. At Anuradhapura (below and right) the Queen saw the inner sanctum of the Sri Lankan Buddhist religion, and the Duke admired a 40-foot statue of Buddha. Ceremonial umbrellas accompanied them at Kandy (opposite and bottom), though the Queen carried her own as well.

with the difficulties facing conservationists. It was a fascinating journey which acquainted him with problems as diverse as the use of chemical fertilisers near natural habitats in Austria and the reintroduction of captive oryx into the wild in Oman. Without even attempting to put his foot in it, he found himself caught up in controversy: in Germany he kept a delicate balance of views when faced with a virulent argument over the pros and cons of building a dyke, and in Sri Lanka he was presented with a baby elephant which London Zoo had to look after at a cost of £3000 a year at a time when it was seeking £1 million in aid from the Government to stay in the black. A reader of the Guardian saw an even more fundamental irony. "The Duke of Edinburgh," she said incredulously, "President of the World Wildlife Fund, is given a young elephant, that will be kept at London Zoo?"

His active involvement with an organisation such as the WWF compelled him to justify his pursuit of game and his support for blood sports, when challenged by journalists who found his interests irreconcilable. His answer was simple: he was concerned about the extinction of species, and the blood sports he patronised did not contribute to such extinction. "Stags need to be culled. Foxes have to be controlled. People who eat beef are not doing any damage to the species cow," he said in March. He was more concerned in May for the future of the whale in the South Atlantic, imagining that many must have been killed in the course of the Falklands conflict because "modern sonar is unable to distinguish between a sub and a whale."

Away from the controversial, the Duke continued to follow his favourite interests during the year. The Duke of Edinburgh Award Scheme reached its Silver Jubilee at the end of 1981 and still the cheques kept coming in. In November he held an exhibition of thirty-six of his own paintings at Sotheby's to raise another few hundred pounds for this most successful of royal ventures. August of that year found him competing again at Cowes and in May 1982 he achieved a decade-long ambition to win the international carriage-driving championships at the Windsor Horse Show – "the most satisfying win of my career," he called it, and off he went to attempt

once again to complete his own book on the art and science of four-in-hand driving. Though he is not a professional sportsman he defended the growth of professionalism in sport. "It is human nature to want to turn personal talents to financial advantage," he told an Olympic Congress at Baden-Baden in September 1981, and he went on to support the role of television and commercial sponsorship.

In April, directly after accompanying the Queen in Canada, Prince Philip travelled to Seattle to be the first "outsider" to test-fly the new Boeing 757 jetliner. After the 90-minute flight, he adjudged it "a very good airplane," though he admitted that "the little black boxes did most of the work." That may have been a good thing in view of the incident the previous November when, as he was flying one of the Andovers of the Queen's flight, he was involved in a near miss

Kandy's torchlight *perahera* was probably the most spectacular tribute to her presence the Queen had seen for years. The whole town was lit up – as were the elephants, with batteries mounted on their heads to service the festoons of coloured lights down their trunks. Dancers and bands celebrated into the early hours.

with a jumbo-jet carrying two hundred passengers from Florida to London. An enquiry established that his aircraft was to blame and that he was at the controls. The following month, when his chauffeur was at the controls of his famous green Bedford electric van, the van collided with a parked car as it was being manoeuvred into position near the Connaught Rooms. Suddenly it seemed the Duke couldn't win. Presumably he puts it down to one of those quirks of Providence similar to that which allows him to be easily the busiest male member of the Royal Family and yet deprived of any constitutional standing, other than the nebulous one of "husband of the Queen."

# Prince Charles

If it was anybody's year in particular there can be no doubt that it belonged to the Prince and Princess of Wales. Their courtship, one of the most public ever for a member of the Royal Family, had been closely followed by the world's press, goaded on by armies of readers and viewers for whom the long-awaited conclusion of Prince Charles' twelve-year search for a bride seemed to justify even the more questionable episodes of public interest. Lady Diana Spencer was, at the time of her engagement, the world's most celebrated unknown quantity and the critics had been ready to pounce on the smallest indiscretion she might unwittingly commit.

But the public thought differently and nothing Lady Diana did could be wrong. She stuck to her own brand of social behaviour – natural, informal, totally spontaneous at all times – made no attempt to conceal her ignorance of protocol and offered no concessions to the dictates of royal fashion. In the five months up to her wedding she had not so much created as publicised her own favourite fashion-

The fascination of an immense project. The Queen inspected the Victoria Dam project at Pogolla, and took her own pictures of the British-financed enterprise (opposite page). Later she and Prince Philip visited a local botanical garden: the Duke planted a tree (below right) and the Queen received an orchid named after her.

notes – the low shoes, the long dresses, the ubiquitous ruffle around neck and wrist. Above all she seemed the perfect complement to a Prince who, despite his wide, growing interest in all manner of things going on around him, looked, dressed and behaved with typical royal conservatism as often as not. If he was not besotted by her he was clearly very much in love with her, and she has been credited with bringing about some softening of his life style.

In a twelve-month period that began with their wedding and ended with the christening of their first child, they were rarely out of the news and much of the lingering interest, never far below the surface, was due to the glow of achievement and satisfaction which their brilliant and superlative wedding had left. Everyone knew it would be everything it was, and hoped and prayed that nothing would go wrong. It didn't. Thanks to the most efficient, military-style planning by Lord Maclean, who received a public kiss from the Princess afterwards, the whole day ran on like clockwork. Only the bolting of a couple of horses and the collapse of two soldiers from

the heat was unplanned, as was the virtual lack of any anti-social behaviour. Not a boo, not a hiss, not a placard out of place spoiled this supreme statement of the British ability to stage-manage a massive ceremonial event for domestic and foreign consumption alike.

The Prince of Wales played his part – naturally: no-one expected otherwise. But his lady's performance won the day. From the cool, modest, almost intimate beginnings, when smiling demurely, huddled in the glass coach, she left Clarence House, to the triumphant drive to Waterloo Station to begin the perfect honeymoon, she captured every heart. Her composure, even as she supported her father on his

Barely an evening went by in the four-day visit to Sri Lanka without a formal evening dinner. (Bottom) the Queen at a Government reception on her first evening: three days later she returned the compliment by giving her own banquet at the Oberoi Hotel, Colombo (right and below). Her departure on 25th October (opposite) was as ceremonial as her arrival.

uncertain walk with her up the aisle of St Paul's, was almost mechanical, yet her little mistake in the order of Prince Charles' name showed that she was as vulnerable, and probably inwardly as nervous, as any other bride on her wedding day. For all that everything went so well the relief was evident as the Prince and Britain's new Princess emerged onto the balcony of Buckingham Palace with their families and the cluster of attendants. Everybody urged them to kiss each other, and read all sorts of meaning into it when they obliged. It was just a bit of a lark and merely confirmed their already evident happiness.

It was a long time before the effect of such a memorable day wore off. The three day stay at Broadlands was accorded total privacy but their progress from Romsey to Eastleigh Airport on 1st August and their ecstatic drive through Gibraltar after they arrived

to board *Britannia* were dutifully recorded for posterity. Press agencies chartered ships and bribed ship owners for news of the royal couple's whereabouts, but their destinations were secret until after the event, and for twelve days they soaked up the sun on the Greek Islands, before calling in on President and Mme Sadat at Cairo and Hurghada.

Their return to Balmoral was fêted every bit as much as their departure from Eastleigh, but a tactful move to invite the Press up for a photo-call in mid-August seemed to have the desired effect and they were left very much alone in their Highland retreat. The news

that their first public round of engagements together as man and wife would be accorded to Wales provoked great excitement in the Principality and preparations for a universal tribute to the new Princess, and no-one was disappointed when it all happened. The three-day tour at the end of October was as comprehensive as possible, taking in North Wales on the first day, mid Wales on the second and the South on the third. Every arm was outstretched in the hope of the briefest hand-clasp and hordes of children lined the narrow streets of over a dozen Welsh towns. Rain – and it came down heavily on the second day – failed to deter either the visitors or their public and at the end of the tour the Princess, very much thrown in at the deep end with such a hectic start to a very public life, must have felt she had earned the Freedom of Cardiff they awarded her on the final evening.

That day she and the Prince had visited a maternity hospital and

All Wales took their new Princess to its heart when she visited over a dozen Welsh communities from 27th to 29th October. Prince Charles paid tribute to her a week later.

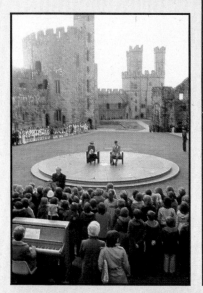

talked a great deal about babies. The Princess paid a lot of attention to the expectant and nursing mothers and Prince Charles was recorded praising the practice of having husbands present at their wives' confinements. It was considered almost too indecent to attribute a possible royal pregnancy to this remark, and the universal

The Duchess of Kent (below) and her sister-in-law Princess Michael combined sophistication and solemnity at the Festival of Remembrance on 7th November.

surprise was all the greater when the official announcement came on 5th November that the Princess was expecting a child. That morning both prospective parents attended a luncheon given by the Lord Mayor at the Guildhall and the occasion was transformed into one of congratulation and emotion. The Lord Mayor spoke of babies as "bits of stardust blown from the hand of God" and Prince Charles, patently moved by the fervour of the occasion, dropped every intention of formality and spoke in conversational terms about "the wonderful effect my dear wife has had on everyone."

If the courtship of this popular royal couple had been intensely public, their forthcoming parenthood was even more so. From the public a supply of gifts, toys and mementos flowed into Buckingham Palace with a persistence which made it necessary to set up a

Wreath-layings the following day at the Cenotaph elicited no smiles. The Princess of Wales, now known to be pregnant, watched from a balcony with the Queen Mother, Princess Alice and King Olav of Norway.

separate office. From the Press there came a never-ending stream of speculation and advice on every aspect of pregnancy, motherhood, fatherhood and baby-care. Hardly any subject was too intimate to discuss, though on the whole the tone was respectful and healthy, if a little trivial at times.

But the Press were by no means faultless during this period and if there was one thing that heightened the joyful anticipation of the Prince and Princess' first child it was the over-zealous, slightly prurient interest of the newspapers. Buckingham Palace, rather ingenuously, had expected public interest to fall away after the wedding but, of course, the latest announcement put paid to that. What angered not only "the Palace" but more specifically the Queen herself was the growing tendency for the Press to pursue the Prince and Princess into the realms of their private lives. The royal couple moved into Highgrove House in a permanent way in early November and photographers hid in bushes to take pictures of them whenever they appeared in the grounds. One series of photographs – harmless enough except for the invasion of privacy which had been necessary to secure them – prompted the Queen to call editors of Fleet Street newspapers to Buckingham Palace in December for a dressing down.

Memories of the old days, as Prince Charles visited *HMS Osprey* on 11th December (below and below right). New experience for Sir Christopher Leaver (right) who as Lord Mayor welcomed the Queen to a carol concert in the City on 17th December.

One editor refused to attend and another was reported to have made it clear to the Queen that any view of the Royal Family from a public access is fair game for the photographer's lens and that he would continue his work accordingly.

How far that criterion was honoured when in February the Prince and Princess took a ten-day holiday in the Bahamas as the

guests of Lord and Lady Romsey was not in doubt after two British newspapers, the *Sun* and the *Daily Star,* published photographs of them dressed only in bathing gear enjoying the sun and sea air on what was fondly imagined to be a private beach. The pictures

The Princess of Wales looked stunning at Guildford, when she and the Prince visited the Cathedral a week before Christmas to attend a Christmas Celebration put on by the Prince's Trust.

showing the Princess of Wales visibly pregnant in her bikini were of course most prominently shown, and Buckingham Palace – supported this time by MPs, the public and, eventually, the Press Council – deplored the standard of professional conduct and voiced the Queen's anxiety, as a mother-in-law rather than as sovereign, for the Princess of Wales' privacy at a time of possible stress. Under this pressure both newspapers quickly apologised for their actions in sending out photographers specifically to pry into the seclusion of the royal couples holiday haunt, though the tone of the apology left

something to be desired in terms of sincerity.

Signs of the "stress" that the Palace had obliquely referred to were of course always being watched for. There is nothing more logical to a journalist who has followed and encouraged a fairy-tale romance with its wonderful wedding than to probe for signs that the bubble has burst. Accordingly, no sooner had the excitement of the Royal Wedding worn off than all manner of reports of dissension in the Windsor camp occupied the gossip columns and even the front pages of the Press. In the year since she returned from honeymoon, the Princess of Wales has been alleged to have become bored with a stiff, formal Court life, argued vehemently with Prince Charles over blood sports, refused gifts from the Queen, insisted on taking her baby with her on any tours she may undertake abroad, been

responsible for the sacking of Prince Charles' valet, as well as of two of her own personal detectives, and for the cooling of relationships between Prince Charles and some of his former friends. In a backlash against the fond myth of her modesty and vulnerability, journalists and authors called evidence from nowhere to show that from the age of sixteen she had nurtured an ambition to hook the Prince of Wales, and had almost gleefully watched her elder sister, Lady Sarah McCorquodale, commit a succession of mistakes during her friendship with him – mistakes from which she then learned how to achieve her ambition. Suddenly she was no longer vulnerable, no longer in need of protection or advice from anyone.

In general terms this was probably not far from the truth, though the specific allegations remain bereft of any sort of satisfactory evidence. Even by, say, March 1982, the Princess had, remarkably, acquired a confidence in all her public appearances that was probably quite unthinkable at the equivalent stage in the previous year, when that black taffeta dress with its low-cut neckline appeared for the first and only time. Clearly under the direction of the Queen's

Prince and Princess Michael of Kent (right) inaugurated *Maritime England* for the English Tourist Board, with a concert at St Paul's Cathedral on 14th January. Princess Alexandra's early duties in 1982 included a fashion show (bottom) in aid of the Mental Health Foundation on 25th January and a visit to the British Museum's *Excavating Egypt* exhibition on 17th February (below).

senior Lady-in-Waiting, Lady Susan Hussey, she had been well schooled in matters royal and her complete indifference to the putting on of airs and graces has made it easier for her to feel at ease. Once she was married she seemed to take lessons from no-one – indeed it may fairly be said that other members of the Royal Family young enough to learn new tricks have taken a few leaves out of her book.

For obvious reasons her public engagements in 1982 were few and far between, though in yet another break with traditional practice for royal mothers-to-be, she appeared, proudly pregnant, on official duties until within five weeks of Prince William's birth – on the last occasion opening a community centre in Deptford as Patron of the Albany Trust, one of five positions of patronage she had assumed the

46

Princess Alice celebrated her eightieth birthday on Christmas Day, and received a new rose, BLESMA Soul, as a belated birthday tribute on 6th January (below and right). Her zest for life continues unabated: (bottom) at Crosby Hall, Chelsea on 17th March.

previous February. Her encounters with the public on all such occasions were spontaneous and in essence delightfully trivial, but they performed the important function of contact – more than merely a presence or a fixed smile, it was contact by touch and by word of mouth. Her manner ("style" or "approach" sounds far too technical and artificial) extended the thinking behind the concept of the walkabout. She did more than merely get close to people. She came to them almost on their terms. Every parent wanted to shake her hand. Every young child wanted to kiss her – and many did. In allowing it to happen she had already set the Royal Family in the direction it should go to survive the continuous process of reappraisal which might otherwise bode ill for the next century.

Prince Charles has not been entirely unaffected by this process and in the last year has probably given more impromptu interviews as he got in and out of cars than he has ever done before. It made nonsense of the old directive "The Royal Family do not give interviews" and both this and his relaxed and open conversational

The Duchess of Kent attended the Penlee Memorial Service at Mousehole on 22nd January.

manner with anonymous people in crowds has added to the relevance the monarchy has for them. If anything he is regarded as one of the more evidently sensitive members of the Royal Family and concern runs through his curriculum vitae like a thread. In January 1982 he cut short his winter holiday to visit parts of Wales which had been badly hit by prolonged and heavy snow. In July he was the first to visit the hospitals where casualties of the Falklands campaign lay wounded, and he lost no time in becoming the Patron of the South Atlantic Fund. In March he and the Princess of Wales suddenly changed plans in order to visit Newcastle and Huddersfield and meet some of the plucky people who, with the aid of cash grants from the Prince's Trust – his idea – have been able to lift themselves from the hopelessness of unemployment into an active and constructive frame of mind.

Experience and youth: the Queen Mother opened Canada House's new cultural centre on 2nd February (this page). The same evening, the Prince and Princess of Wales visited 11 Downing Street (opposite).

The year will probably be best remembered, were it not for the birth of their child, as the year in which Prince Charles stayed at home. If one of the most common impressions of his life-style in the last dozen years has been one of a genial globe-trotter, it changed after his marriage. There was not a single official trip abroad, save for a day's visit to France on the eve of Prince William's birth, and because of that impending birth the original plans for him and the Princess to visit Australia and Canada were postponed. The Prince seemed to become an utterly domesticated man, less restless than he was reported to be as a bachelor, and less impatient of the system that forces him to wait for many years before his long apprenticeship ends.

But he found other interests. His polo kept him fit and active and rarely a week-end went by, before or after the birth of his son, where he was not engaged to play in two or three hard fought matches. The occasional fall from a pony and a nasty blow on the mouth from a polo mallet failed to put him off the sport in which he has already exceeded his father's high standards. His wife, long saddled with the allegation that she does not enjoy watching him risk his neck on the polo field, nailed it, both by word and by deed, and her

A quiet celebration of thirty years as Queen: Elizabeth II and her consort at Sandringham early in February 1982. Second son Prince Andrew (below) would soon be off to prove himself in the South Atlantic: third son Prince Edward (below centre) was about to celebrate his coming-of-age, and to contemplate life in New Zealand.

presence on the side-lines, in increasingly voluminous maternity smocks, was as newsworthy as any goal from an impossible angle. Together they also went to the races – at Cheltenham on Gold Cup day the Princess seemed out of sorts and at odds with everyone, including her husband, and rumours of a pretty substantial tiff flared up in no time. But two weeks later they were at Aintree to watch the Grand National and the appearances changed. She was animated and interested, chatting constantly to her companion, Mrs Nick Gaselee, and when Prince Charles took her down to the Canal Turn to watch the field jumping one of the highest fences, she clambered up with him onto the bonnet of their Range Rover. For obvious reasons, the Press were back on their side.

All in all the year has been a hectic one for both partners, and it is certainly difficult to envisage anything like it on the same very personal scale for many years to come. Ahead of them lie a lot of "firsts" – their first foreign tour, their first outing with Prince William, their first really full year of public engagements uninterrupted by personal and domestic affairs. How each, or both, will fare is now much more certain than it could ever have been a year ago. Prince Charles is settled, his wife has arrived. It must surely be comparatively plain sailing from now on.

# Prince Andrew

In the shadow of the brilliant events in the life of the Prince and Princess of Wales, the Queen's second son looked set for a quiet sort of year pursuing his career in the Royal Navy. Although he was seen

at public events – escorting his future sister-in-law to the Trooping in June, and acting as his brother's senior supporter the following month – his career, two years old in September 1981, took up most of his time.

His reputation as a ladies' man lost nothing of its momentum, however, as fresh rumours of ephemeral liaisons, and various public sightings were reported. One such report alleged that he had invited the Princess of Wales' former flat-mate, Carolyn Pride, to Balmoral in September, but the friendship did not develop. Another rumour arose from a claim made by Lindsay Ross, a model who burst in upon a dinner party he gave in February at the London restaurant, Mimme d'Ischia, and smothered him with kisses. A second model, Joanne Latham revealed in April that she had shared an "intimate candlelight dinner" with Prince Andrew, but later confessed that her

(Opposite page) the Queen at the British Institute of Radiology on 11th February (centre), and opening the Alexandra Wing of the London Hospital on 24th March (far left). On 23rd February, the Queen Mother attended a thanksgiving service at St Peter's Walworth (right).

Meanwhile the Duke of Edinburgh's World Wildlife Fund tour took him to India (below and below right) and Port Sudan (remaining pictures) and eight other countries in February and March.

story was untrue. The most positive indication of any friendship came when in January he went to see the musical *Cats* in London, with an unknown blonde. The Press identified her later as the ballet dancer Karen Paisey and her own mother seemed to confirm the story, but Karen denied that she was the Prince's companion that night and said she had never met him.

Prince Andrew was now at the age (he celebrated his 22nd birthday on 19th February) when, but for his Service career, public duties would normally take over, and indeed his first solo engagement took place on 8th December. He attended the one hundredth Varsity Rugby match at Twickenham and as guest of honour presented the Cups and medals after the game. The match had been preceded by some of the heaviest December snow for some years and the presentations were enlivened by groups of spectators running onto the pitch to hurl snowballs up at the royal guest. He took it all in superb sporting spirit, though he probably yearned for the chance to retaliate. He attended a dinner to celebrate the anniversary that evening at the Hilton Hotel in London and gave his first public speech there.

On 6th February Prince Andrew represented the Queen at the wedding of Princess Marie-Astrid of Luxemburg and Archduke Charles Christian of Hapsburg, a member of the old Austro-Hungarian imperial family. It was one of three royal weddings in Luxemburg in the space of thirteen months – in February 1981 the heir, Prince Henri, married a girl of Brazilian descent, and in March

1982 Princess Margaretha married Prince Nicholas of Liechtenstein. The wedding of Princess Marie-Astrid was of particular interest in Britain because it was she who was hotly tipped in 1977 as a bride for the Prince of Wales. Perhaps it was for this reason that Prince Charles did not attend the ceremonies in Luxemburg, but Prince Andrew's presence caused a little bit of speculation too. As the escort of Princess Elena, daughter of King Juan Carlos of Spain, he was not only credited with smoothing over the so-called rift between the British and Spanish royal families following the Prince and Princess of Wales' honeymoon, but was also reported to have got on so well with her that more rumours of an impending courtship began to develop.

Events, however, began to overtake as developments abroad contrived to make 1982 Prince Andrew's most exciting year to date and, furthermore, it was all inextricably linked with his chosen career. In January he had joined 820 Helicopter Squadron on board the 19,500-ton submarine-hunter *HMS Invincible* after his final and

The Duchess of Gloucester sailed into her tenth year as a member of the Royal Family with a confident appearance as guest of honour at the Ambassadorial Ball Soirée Française at Grosvenor House on 22nd February. Eric Morecambe provided some of the fun.

successfully completed training as an operational and qualified helicopter pilot. In fact he experienced more than simple training the previous September when AB John Hendren was swept overboard from the submarine *HMS Ocelot* by a freak wave in the Firth of Clyde and Prince Andrew's helicopter, on a training exercise a few hundred yards away, was assigned to the rescue. Manoeuvring the controls to effect a perfect rescue under the supervision of his commanding officer, Prince Andrew won praise from a Navy spokesman for acting "in the manner expected of a Royal Naval helicopter pilot," and from the Ministry of Defence who said, "Prince Andrew seems to have

A brush with the Press did not seem to spoil the Prince and Princess of Wales' holiday in the Bahamas, and they returned to London Airport with the Romseys on 27th February (below right). A visit to the Barbican Centre followed on 4th March (below).

acted in a very cool fashion."

His tour on the *Invincible* was due to last for two years and began with a ten-day spell of manoeuvres off the north-west coast of Scotland. He was thrilled with the ship and, using the most overworked of royal epithets, said, "She's marvellous," as he came ashore for weekend leave at Rosyth at the end of February. The Queen and Prince Edward were due to visit him on board at the end of March but by then the Falklands dispute was close at hand, and on 3rd April Prince Andrew was recalled from short leave at Windsor Castle to join a thousand officers and men in readiness for possible war.

The advisability of putting members of the Royal Family into the theatre of war is for all sorts of reasons never cut and dried, but it was soon made clear that there was never any doubt that Prince Andrew should go. A statement from Buckingham Palace

emphasised that "if *Invincible* is in action, then Prince Andrew will be too. The Prince answered the call like any other serviceman and left immediately. He is a serving officer and there was no question in the Queen's mind that he should go." So, on 4th April, standing smartly to attention on the deck of his ship, he sailed from Portsmouth harbour as *Invincible* led a flotilla of Task Force ships out into the Atlantic to the accompaniment of cheers from thousands of wellwishers, the clatter of escorting helicopters and bursts of red flares sent up in salute.

There was plenty of work to be done as the force headed for the Falklands, and Prince Andrew enjoyed no privileges. "There are no special instructions," confirmed his commanding officer Lt-Cdr Wykes-Sneyd. "If any decision is made, it would obviously come from higher up the line. He gets no quarter from his colleagues and competes extremely well with them." In mid-April the *Invincible* crossed the line and Prince Andrew got the usual treatment – a ducking from his colleagues – just as his forebears had in their day. By then, however, preparations for a war which now seemed inevitable were being made in earnest and Prince Andrew was making regular trial sorties in his Sea King helicopter.

Once into South Atlantic waters Prince Andrew was not kept waiting for action. His first taste of war's grim realities came towards the end of April when he took part in an abortive search for Petty Officer Kevin Casey whose helicopter ditched during a night reconnaissance flight. Just over a week later he was flying low over the blazing ruins of *HMS Sheffield,* the first and thus the most famous

of the Argentine's victims, helping in the frantic yet efficient search for, and rescue of, survivors. During the remainder of his time at sea, until the British victory early in June gave him the opportunity to set foot on the Falkland Islands he had helped to liberate, he was, as Buckingham Palace put it, "on front line duty round the clock," acting as a decoy for the notoriously effective "fire and forget" Exocet missiles, which wrought great damage to British ships and was the enemy's very best weapon. In the wake of suspicions that Prince Andrew was being kept back from front line activity, the Queen made

Prince Charles visited Westonbirt Arboretum, Gloucestershire on 5th March. His wife met Elizabeth Taylor three days later at the première of *The Little Foxes* in London.

an exception to her usual reticence about such matters, and authorised an official statement confirming that "neither operational requirements, nor indeed Prince Andrew, would tolerate his being singled out for special treatment. He and his colleagues have had a very active month since the military action began."

In spite of a regular supply of letters from the family back home – although no special facilities for delivery were accorded – and a wealth of good luck messages from listeners to the British Forces

Radio, Prince Andrew spent what he later admitted was on occasions a terrifying time in the South Atlantic, and he would not have been tremendously consoled by Prince Charles' reminder that while "I feel a bit sorry for him being tossed about on the high seas, at least he can get off the ship in his helicopter occasionally."

The *Invincible* stayed in the South Atlantic for three months after the Falklands' recapture and Prince Andrew was obliged to miss the christening of Prince William whose birth had been regarded almost as the jewel in the crown of success in the Falklands. When eventually the *Invincible* returned in September the Queen, Prince Philip and Princess Anne went to meet him. And he announced that the first thing he wanted, now that he was back home, was a pint of milk.

# Prince Edward

Naturally it was less easy for schoolboy Prince Edward to enjoy quite as exciting a year as his elder brother but 1982 in particular brought about a number of significant and fundamental changes in his life. No date was more symbolic of those changes than 10th March, the day he celebrated his 18th birthday and coming-of-age.

"Celebrated" may not be quite the right word, because like any other pupil whose birthday falls on a schoolday, the Prince spent his at his desk. But the Queen had sent a cake up to Gordonstoun which helped to tide him over until he could celebrate in more traditional style with a family get-together during the Easter holidays.

Like most major royal anniversaries, Prince Edward's coming-of-age was marked by the publication of a series of photographs, taken late in January in the grounds of Buckingham Palace by Tim Graham. The growing informal style of such portraits was perpetuated, the Prince wearing a casual jacket that had been handed down by Prince Andrew and a pair of corduroy trousers that

had been visibly let down by a Palace seamstress to cater for his rapidly increasing height. With him in some photographs was his black Labrador bitch Frances, while other pictures showed him in his somewhat cluttered study sitting at a desk with a mug which bore the legend, "Old photographers never die, they just fade away." One in the eye for someone.

No official information was available about his birthday presents but, coincidentally, the Chancellor of the Exchequer released news the previous day that as part of the Civil List increases for 1982

A thunderbolt and a suspiciously parked car threatened to take the shine off the Sultan of Oman's State Visit to Britain on 16th March, but all went well enough. The Kents and Gloucesters (opposite, far left) were among the royal welcoming party.

Prince Edward would receive £20,000 per annum – or £16,183 between his coming of age and the end of the calendar year. In fact only 5% of the total would be available to him, as a contribution towards secretarial expenses, the remainder being invested until his public duties begin.

Those duties seemed to be as far away as ever because the following month, while he was enjoying a 10-day holiday with a group of friends in the Austrian Tyrol, it was announced that on leaving Gordonstoun in the middle of July he would take up a post as house tutor and junior master at the Collegiate School at Wanganui, on New Zealand's North Island. The school, which boasts a complement of 525 boys and fees of £2000 a year, was founded in 1854 by a Yorkshire missionary and is now run on traditional academic lines, embracing a leaning towards the classics, a good reputation for rowing and rugby, a fagging system and an emphasis on good manners and appearance. Prince Edward would be responsible for the supervision of seventy or so boys of various ages, and for assisting with their hobbies, outdoor activities, extra-mural studies and cultural work. He might also be allowed to teach, though only under supervision.

The school's headmaster Mr Ian McKinnon was thrilled with the

The Queen planted a tree at the Staff College at Camberley on 19th March. (Bottom pictures and opposite page) guests at the Sultan of Oman's banquet at Claridge's on 18th March: Princess Anne and Captain Mark Phillips. The Queen is greeted personally by the Sultan.

choice, which was believed to have originated from the pupil exchange scheme that flourishes between Gordonstoun and Wanganui, and said, "The masters and boys feel honoured that the school should be chosen. I think Prince Edward will fit in very well. He is a young man with a wide range of interests."

If anyone wanted evidence of that "wide range of interests" – Prince Edward is already well-known for his love of sailing, ski-ing and horse-riding – it came in a surprise announcement in mid-May that he wished to be considered for recruitment into the Royal Marines. To assurances from Buckingham Palace that his ambition in this direction was a long-term venture, he took three days' secondment from Gordonstoun to attend an officer assessment course at the Royal Marine Commando Training Centre at Lympstone, in Devon. Here he was briefed about the life-style of a commando and told that a two-year minimum course would involve twelve months' basic training and a further twelve months' active commando training. In addition he underwent a two-day endurance course designed, as they put it, to test every muscle in the body.

So, on 18th and 19th May the Prince was put through his paces in much the same way as his elder brothers had been before him: Prince Andrew, who in 1980 spent a fortnight at it, had described it as "two

Princess Margaret (below) and the Duchess of Gloucester (opposite page far right) arrive for the Sultan's banquet on 18th March. A week earlier, Princess Margaret opened the Burlington House Fair (right), and on 12th March Princess Anne inspected a Sandhurst passing-out parade.

weeks of hell." In those two days Prince Edward shinned up trees, leapt over tank traps, scrambled over a six-foot wall, slid down a rope – "the Death Slide" – from a 50-foot tower, crawled through pipe tunnels, struggled over rope-nets and carried a man for five hundred yards in a fireman's lift. And, apart from a distinct impression of exhaustion, the worst he got was a bloody nose. His instructors thought he came through "pretty well," which didn't surprise his Gordonstoun headmaster Mr Michael Mavor. "He has taken part in plenty of adventure expeditions," he commented, "and enters into things wholeheartedly."

That was during Prince Edward's last term at Gordonstoun. Prince Andrew sent a telegram to him to wish him "the best of British luck" for his A-levels, which he took in History, English and Politics with Economics. Shortly before he left for Wanganui in September the results were announced, and showed that Prince Edward had finished his school career a class or two above his brothers – all 'A' levels passed and one with a distinction. It more than justifies the opinion of Mr Mavor who on 11th July, when the Queen came to Gordonstoun to fetch her son home on his last day,

said: "He has done very well indeed. He is a very good all-rounder. He has had a very successful school career and we are all proud to have had him here."

# Princess Anne

It was something of a historical coincidence that Princess Anne, whose wedding on 14th November 1973 eclipsed the Prince of Wales'

25th birthday celebrations that day, should have chosen 27th July 1981 – just two days before his wedding – for the christening of her daughter. She had been born on 15th May, and all the traditional accoutrements of a royal christening attended her at Buckingham Palace two months later. She was named Zara Anne Elizabeth – Zara means "bright as the dawn" – and the families of each parent assembled for the ceremony. Lord Lichfield took the official pictures which, in deference to the vast publicity then being given to the Prince of Wales and his fiancée, were not released until Princess

Anne's 32nd birthday on 15th August.

By then, not only had she attended the Prince of Wales' wedding, wearing a sharp, bright outfit which matched the brilliance of the occasion, but she had made her first informal public appearance since Zara's birth, at Locko Park Horse Trials in Derbyshire. While the remainder of her family were on holiday at Balmoral, she undertook her first public engagement, on 21st August, at Dartford, for which she used a Wessex V helicopter of the type that only a week before had crashed in the North Sea with the loss of 13 lives.

These two events set the pace and style of her next twelve months' programme and signalled a return to the mixture of public duties and the private pursuit of her most absorbing pastime, three-day eventing, with which she is now unquestionably associated. At home her public engagements continued where she had left off early in the year, but there was great significance in her formal installation as Chancellor of London University on 12th October. Her selection as the successor to her grandmother, Queen Elizabeth the Queen Mother, who held the post for 25 years until 1980, was challenged and Princess Anne found herself contesting the Chancellorship with Jack Jones, the former Trades Union Leader, and Nelson Mandela, the imprisoned champion of the rights of black South Africans. In the event, Princess Anne won the vote easily and another, no doubt lengthy royal presidency began. A fortnight later, by coincidence, Princess Anne, as guest of honour at the Women of the Year luncheon at the Savoy, met Mrs Robert Mugabe, wife of the

Prince Philip in hilarious mood at a charity dinner in London on 17th March. The Duchess of Gloucester, in Southampton to see *Evil Under the Sun* on 25th March, is suitably more restrained.

first black leader of the new state of Zimbabwe whose independence had been granted by Prince Charles on behalf of the Queen the previous year.

One of Princess Anne's more hazardous engagements was a two-day visit to Northern Ireland – her first since 1977 – in March. Travelling from one venue to another in a bullet-proof car, she carried out a full programme of duties, which included an investiture at Hillsborough Castle, a dinner with the Northern Ireland Secretary James Prior, visits to the Royal Corps of Signals, of which she is

Colonel-in-Chief, and inspections of projects by the Save the Children Fund of which she is President. Thanks to tight security throughout, she survived the tour without untoward incident. The year was not devoid of other incidents, however: in November she had faced a hostile demonstration protesting against blood sports when she opened a slaughter-house in Edinburgh. Anti-blood sports supporters merged with vegetarians to provide such a noisy backdrop to the occasion that the Princess must have wondered why she bothered. But, with that practised coolness which is the hallmark of royalty, she pretended not to notice, as she did again in Manchester the following April when demonstrators protested against the South African links fostered by the firm in Wythenshawe whose factory she was about to open.

Princess Anne spent a month or so of the year abroad. In November she was greeted at Katmandu by Princess Sharada, a sister of King Birendra, at the beginning of a ten-day visit to Nepal to see

the work of national and local organisations of the Save the Children
Fund and she followed this with a short courtesy visit to New Delhi.
In June she paid a week's visit to the United States, visiting Denver,
Colorado, where she looked in on the set of the famous TV series
"Dynasty," and Houston, Texas. This tour seemed to be fraught with
all sorts of difficulties and did nothing to improve Princess Anne's
reputation as one susceptible to sudden outbursts of ill-temper. No
doubt an over-zealous Press took every possible liberty with the
comparative informality of the tour, but the Princess was palpably
irked by their familiarity and hustle, and she upset many Americans
by her constant scowling and cold-shouldering. The worst moment
came when news of Prince William's birth was announced to her by a
journalist anxious to record her immediate reaction. "Oh, how nice,"
replied Princess Anne, almost sarcastically, and sparked off
immediate rumours that she was jealous, or didn't see eye-to-eye

with her sister-in-law, or whatever. The Queen was reported to have taken her to task over the incident, but it is more likely that Princess Anne's reaction was directed against the American Press and not an indication of her relationship with the Princess of Wales, and that within the family the affair blew over quite amicably.

A much happier visit to Canada followed the next month, when Princess Anne spent a fortnight touring the Yukon, Saskatchewan, Manitoba and Ottawa – again primarily as President of SCF. In the Yukon, she visited the Whitehorse mine, 700 feet underground, and was highly amused at the oversized protective suit they gave her to

Pot-pourri of royal engagements: Princess Margaret took the Sovereign's Parade at Sandhurst on 10th April; the Duchess of Kent attended a concert at Merchant Taylor's Hall on 17th March; the Princess of Wales returned to Kings Cross Station after a visit to Leeds on 30th March, and the Queen opened Shire Hall, Reading on 2nd April.

wear. With massive boots, protective goggles and a thick helmet, she cut a strange figure as she carried a bouquet to the head of the mineshaft! She visited Regina in Saskatchewan, saw a glacier from Kluano National Park and had dinner with Prime Minister Trudeau in Ottawa. But one personal tribute to her failed to come off: her visit to Winnipeg Races to watch the Princess Anne Stakes was called off at two hours' notice, because the racecourse company had run into financial difficulties and had closed down to prevent further losses.

Princess Anne, and her husband Captain Mark Phillips, enjoyed only moderate success in competitions around the country's three-day event courses. Captain Phillips continued to prosper from the controversial sponsoring arrangement he had concluded with Range

Rover in 1980, since when he has received some £70,000 in sponsor fees and over £10,000 in prize money. In March 1982 he negotiated an extension of the agreement until the end of 1983, with a two-year option to follow, and this effectively rid him of any financial worries in the long preparatory period before the Los Angeles Olympics in 1984.

For all that it was not his best year. It was badly interrupted by a slack period over Christmas when he overdid the relaxation necessary to overcome back troubles, and found he had put on 1½ stone by the end of January. He had been unplaced at the Burghley Horse Trials the previous September – like Princess Anne, he fell into a ditch – and his chances in the Martell Cognac Championship at Upminster in January were thwarted by bad weather which scuppered his transport arrangements. At the Badminton Horse Trials he withdrew his Olympic hope, Classic Lines, after an excellent performance in the cross country phase, on the grounds he did not

The Prince and Princess of Wales made friends with Merseyside during a visit to open the Chinese quarter's community centre on 2nd April.

want to reduce the horse's self-confidence by asking too much of him. Nevertheless he came 14th out of almost eighty competitors at Badminton, he had won £1500 prize money at Wylye Horse Trials near Salisbury the previous October, and he made a modest but successful venture into journalism in April when he began writing an occasional column in the new Sunday newspaper *The Mail on Sunday*. "The view from the saddle," he said, "is often quite different from that of the critic on the ground."

Princess Anne's return to the saddle was certainly no more

successful than her husband's. She was thrown into lakes and ditches three times – at Burghley, Badminton and Hagley in Worcestershire, and had a furious altercation with photographers at Badminton whom she eventually told to "Naff off." Badminton was also famed this year for the antics of young Peter Phillips, who in a spasm of devilment created all sorts of noise and disorder as he and

an older playmate chased each other round the collecting ring, defying the remonstrations of his parents. Boyish as it may have been, it was not the sort of lark that would have been tolerated at his new school, the £200-a-term Blueboys, near Minchinhampton, which he joined the following month. First impressions were good, "He has settled down well," said headmistress Elspeth Bland.

Aintree at the beginning of April means the Grand National, and the Prince and Princess of Wales couldn't resist the temptation. As if no-one were looking, they clambered onto cars to watch the race.

Two particularly interesting insights into the private and public life of Princess Anne and Captain Phillips were provided by a television interview and a book, both released during the year. The interview, given by Princess Anne for the programme called "The Princess Anne, Her Working Life," did much to project the unseen side of a controversial woman, and in particular to show how fully she participates in the regimented planning of each engagement – including the speeches, all of which she writes herself. She was well aware that her position in line of succession would slip down over the next few years and that her children would not become involved in royal duties.

The book was Angela Rippon's "Mark Phillips; the Man and his Horses." This was a wide-ranging, but by no means comprehensive look at Princess Anne's husband, but it confirmed the general impression of him as a somewhat nervous, retiring man, easily baulked by the prospect of being involved in grandiose royal occasions. He was, understandably perhaps, "petrified" when he asked Prince Philip for Princess Anne's hand in marriage, a request made none the easier by the fact that Prince Philip, who had been abroad for substantial periods, had little inkling that matters had come that far. Captain Phillips was, in his own words, "a nervous heap" at his wedding, and found himself unable to match his father-in-law's wit when his turn came to reply to the toast to the bride and groom. Both he and Princess Anne were sea-sick during the first

Wales received saturation treatment in April with three royal visits in three days. On the 6th, Prince Charles opened the Glamorgan Nature Reserve at Tondu, and on the 7th his wife visited Bridgend to open Sony's new factory.

four days of their honeymoon cruise, and Captain Phillips found it "quite a frightening experience" to be in on the birth of his son in 1977, and unwillingly "co-opted into the proceedings" for the birth of his daughter.

But the book also contained a graphic description, at first hand, of the almost heroic part he played during that night in March 1974 when a mentally unstable gunman attempted to kidnap Princess Anne as she and her husband were being driven to Buckingham

Palace. He spent almost fifteen horrific minutes trying to talk the gunman out of his attempt, and was even engaged in a virtual tug of war with him as he tried to pull the Princess from her seat. With three men lying half-dead in the roadway he did well to prevent, by whatever means, any further bloodshed inside the car.

Angela Rippon, the former BBC TV newsreader, had spent several months with the Phillipses at Gatcombe Park, interviewing them for the purpose of her book. As most of her time collecting material, watching farming procedures, and horseriding, was spent with Captain Phillips, the inevitable rumours of a liaison developed. These were firmly and constantly denied by both parties, but they grew into more persistent speculation about the imminent breakdown of Princess Anne's marriage – and this on evidence no more cogent than the absence of Captain Phillips from most of the official engagements his wife undertook as a member of the Royal Family. It was really quite startling how much notice several sections of the Press took of these regular absences, and how little of the fact that as a working farmer and a top equestrian competitor, he has little choice but to avoid time-consuming public engagements which his wife is perfectly competent, and paid, to perform. Captain Phillips, deploring the constant adverse publicity put it simply in an interview he gave to "The Field" magazine in January: "I try and go

The Queen's peripatetic Maundy patronage brought her this year to St David's Cathedral in mid-Wales. On 8th April she carried out the traditional office of presenting purses to the aged. In this her 56th year, there were fifty-six recipients of either sex.

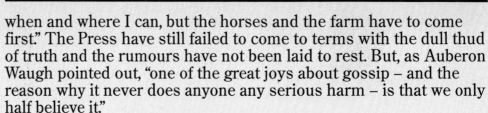

when and where I can, but the horses and the farm have to come first." The Press have still failed to come to terms with the dull thud of truth and the rumours have not been laid to rest. But, as Auberon Waugh pointed out, "one of the great joys about gossip – and the reason why it never does anyone any serious harm – is that we only half believe it."

# The Queen Mother

"The difference a year makes" really sums up the twelve-month period between the Queen Mother's 81st and 82nd birthdays. Her 81st birthday came only six days after the wedding of her senior grandson, the Prince of Wales, to the granddaughter of Lady Fermoy, the senior female member of her household, and in the wake of the expansive publicity of that occasion she decided not to make her usual public birthday appearance at Clarence House. Instead, she spent the day quietly at Sandringham before making for Scotland for the remainder of her summer holiday. Her 82nd birthday could not have been more of a contrast. The Prince and Princess of Wales had,

The Queen Mother charmed and was charmed at the concert which Luciano Pavarotti gave at the Royal Albert Hall on 13th April.

thoughtfully, chosen the day, 4th August, for the christening of Prince William, so not only was the Queen Mother in London to receive her customary accolade from a larger than usual crowd of admirers and wellwishers, but she also experienced the thrill of seeing the ultimate successor to her late husband christened in traditional royal style. Naturally she held the baby for a few minutes, to allow the photographic record of the link between four generations to be made, and just as naturally the baby cried as lustily as ever. The Queen Mother, much amused, said "Well he's certainly got a good pair of lungs, hasn't he?"

In some other ways it was a year of memories. The thirtieth anniversary of the Queen's accession on 6th February was also the thirtieth anniversary of the death of King George VI, and both the Queen and the Queen Mother spent that day as part of their winter break at Sandringham while the guns of the Royal Horse Artillery and the Honourable Artillery Company paid their tributes in London. The previous September, whilst at the Castle of Mey in Scotland, the Queen Mother paid a visit to St John's Episcopal Church at Forfar, on Tayside, where she was confirmed on 5th November 1916. There she met Mrs Margaret Cadenhead, the same age as herself, and Miss Nellie Brymer, a mere youngster at 79, both of whom were confirmed with her. And in March, the Queen Mother took a trip down Memory

Lane with a visit to London's West End to see a gala performance of "Underneath the Arches" – a tribute to Flanagan and Allen, whose stage performances she and King George loved during the forties and fifties.

Sadder memories, for one who lost a brother, a brother-in-law

and a nephew in two World Wars, closed in during early November when the Queen Mother paid her annual tributes to the fallen. On the 6th she planted her Cross in the Royal British Legion's Field of Remembrance at St Margaret's Westminster, standing by that saddening mass of wooden memorials, reminders of the appalling human cost of war. The following day she was present, with the rest of the Royal Family, at the Festival of Remembrance, at which poppies, each representing a life lost in those wars, are showered down from the roof of the Albert Hall. And on the 8th, her wreath was laid for her at the Cenotaph while, with the Princess of Wales, Princess Alice and the King of Norway, she watched the unchanging

Service of Remembrance from a balcony over Whitehall.

But the year brought some happier anniversaries which the Queen Mother, despite her gradually diminishing schedule of engagements, shared. Perhaps the most satisfying for her was the centenary celebration of the Royal College of Music, of which she is President. In November she conferred a Fellowship of the College on the conductor Lorin Maazel, and an honorary doctorate upon the Prince of Wales, and it was Prince Charles who, with the Princess of

Prince and Princess Michael shared some private moments (opposite) at Badminton Horse Trials as Princess Anne, competing for the first time in three years, took an early bath in the cross country.

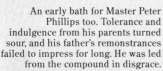

An early bath for Master Peter Phillips too. Tolerance and indulgence from his parents turned sour, and his father's remonstrances failed to impress for long. He was led from the compound in disgrace.

Wales, accompanied her to the centenary thanksgiving service at Westminster Abbey at the end of February.

The centenary of the first shipment of meat from New Zealand to Britain seems a strange one to celebrate, but celebrate it the Queen Mother did, with the happiest of visits to Smithfield Meat Market in London. Londoners have a legendary admiration and love for the Queen Mother and it became transparently evident on this occasion. She entered the massive hall to the spontaneous singing of "Maybe It's Because She's a Londoner," and her tour of the various stallholders brought out the best in them and her. Meat-cutter Gerry Branch told her she looked "lovely," grabbed hold of her hand and kissed it fervently, and the Queen Mother was quietly delighted. 'Some people put on clean aprons," he said afterwards, "but I kept my old one on: I knew she wanted to see us as we really are." She received another kiss from Sean Burridge when she saw his red, white and blue hat and said, "You look very patriotic." As she left they all showered her with flowers. What more could she say than "I've had a wonderful time."

Ceremony and informality blend perfectly each year when the Queen Mother goes to Pirbright to take part in the St Patrick's Day Parade for the Irish Guards, in March. The 1st Battalion were flown from Eire especially for the occasion and the Queen Mother returned

the compliment of having a shamrock pinned on her coat by "awarding" shamrocks to each of the officers. It was the eighteenth time the Queen Mother has taken part in this, probably her favourite ceremony. Significantly, and for obvious reasons, the Queen Mother had not actually visited any of her regiments in Northern Ireland since the current troubles began – indeed not since 1966. But in April

A family at play. Captain Phillips indulged in some early practice for the Trials, but came only 14th. His wife withdrew after her ducking. Prince Edward (below) took a leisurely canter round the grounds while the Queen Mother looked on with the Duke of Beaufort.

she put that right with a visit to the 1st Queen's Dragoon Guards, of which she is Colonel-in-Chief, at their barracks in Omagh, County Tyrone. Like Princess Anne's trip to Northern Ireland the previous month, the Queen Mother's 5-hour visit was kept a secret until it had taken place, and she met soldiers and their families amid tight security.

The Queen Mother left the country only once during the year, for a short visit to Paris in mid-May. Part of the visit was private – she has made private excursions to France in many previous years – but

she also met President Mitterand at the Elysée Palace before carrying out her main engagement of the visit, the opening of a new wing of the British Hartford Hospital at Levallois-Perret. She planted a tree in its garden to commemorate her visit, and three weeks later planted another – a tulip-tree this time – in the Savill Gardens at Windsor Great Park, in commemoration of its Golden Jubilee. These gardens have a special significance for the Queen Mother, since King George VI, an enthusiastic and knowledgeable gardener himself, took a close personal interest in their development after the war.

Her tour of the Cinque Ports was made in June – a customary visit ever since her installation as Lord Warden in August 1979 – but it got off to a poor start. The original scheme for the Queen Mother to sail in *Britannia* had to be abandoned because the arrival time at Ramsgate did not coincide with the tides, and it was arranged that she would leave from Windsor, the day after she met President and

Mrs Reagan there, by helicopter instead. Unfortunately the helicopter, another Wessex, had to make a precautionary landing after an electronic warning light came on in the cockpit. Although the aircraft came down directly and without circling, neither the Queen Mother nor her party were shaken, and they were driven to Heathrow Airport to take a flight to RAF Manston in an Andover. In the event, the royal visits to Ramsgate and Margate were cancelled, but those to Faversham and Canterbury took place as planned.

The Queen Mother's return from her three-day tour was more

auspicious. She sailed in the *Britannia* to Portsmouth on a bright, sunny day, 11th June. On reaching the Solent, *Britannia* passed the *Queen Elizabeth 2* on the last few miles of her voyage from the South Atlantic as one of the requisitioned troopships in the Task Force. The Queen Mother waved in greeting from the deck of *Britannia* and 700 survivors from three ships sunk off the Falklands saluted in return. It was the first of many royal welcomings to homecoming heroes after the successful recapture of the Islands, and in view of her efforts during the First World War to look after wounded soldiers, and her support on the home front during the Second, it was fitting that this lively and active octogenarian should have been off Portsmouth to see the *QE2* in home waters again.

The Queen arrived in Canada for a four-day visit on 15th April (this page), primarily to sign over Britain's last constitutional links with Canada. The formalities included a reception at Government House on 16th April (opposite).

# Princess Margaret

It is a rare year these days when Princess Margaret's private life plays second fiddle to her public duties in the estimation of the Press, and 1981/2 was no exception. An emphatic starting point to yet another exhaustive account of her life and loves was provided by a book, published in October 1981, called "HRH Princess Margaret: A

Life Unfulfilled." It was written by the *Daily Mail* gossip columnist Nigel Dempster, who has kept his readers informed for well over a decade of his version of each stage in Princess Margaret's marriage to, and separation and divorce from, Lord Snowdon; her liaison with Roddy Llewellyn and her quest for fulfilment since it ended. The complete story, with the Townsend affair thrown in as background, was conveniently, and readably, put together in this publication of which, Mr Dempster claimed, the Princess herself had read almost half and which she had approved.

Its revelations, to those who had not kept abreast of events as they had occurred, were many and varied, and dealt as

No hard feelings. The Queen and Prince Philip in the best of humours at Government House Ottawa on 16th April (above), and again during a reception given by the Canadian Premier, Pierre Trudeau, on 17th April (opposite top and left). The Queen also toured Canada's Parliament Buildings during her visit (opposite bottom).

comprehensively with Lord Snowdon's alleged affairs during their marriage as with the many friendships of the Princess herself. The *Daily Mail*, understandably, published a series of lengthy extracts in September and even the *Sunday Telegraph* gave authoritative coverage with an interview with Mr Dempster and some excerpts from the book. That it found a place in the best sellers list for some weeks immediately after its publication testifies to the strong public fascination, for whatever reasons, for an insight into the private life of a Princess who, now a very young 52, has been described during her life by almost every conflicting epithet from beautiful and sophisticated to wayward and unpredictable.

Nevertheless, friends of Princess Margaret were less than happy with the book's allegations, and a bookshop in Knightsbridge at which she has an account refused to stock it. Jocelyn Stevens, one of her life-long friends, published an article in the *Daily Express* casting doubt upon the book's reliability by pointing out a host of what he termed inaccuracies and inconsistencies, and he ended his challenge with this flourish: "In his acknowledgements, Mr Dempster thanks me for introducing him to Princess Margaret. I cannot remember performing such an unfortunate function, but if I did I owe her an immense apology for which I do not expect to be forgiven." Lord Snowdon, more simply, refused to make any comment on the book, which he said had been "written without interviews." The following June he felt compelled to dissociate himself from another book – no

doubt published to cash in on the success of Mr Dempster's – called "Snowdon: A Man For Our Time," a meaningless title which respectably concealed a fairly caustic criticism of what its author David Sinclair considered to be Lord Snowdon's less than creditable part in the breakdown of his marriage with Princess Margaret. Lord Snowdon, who has resolutely refused all inducements to publish his

own memoirs, protested to the book's publisher and said he would make it quite clear that he "had no part in its production whatsoever."

Mr Dempster's book had at least finished on a note of hope, in the form of an assurance that Princess Margaret had now come to terms with things and did not really contemplate a re-marriage that would be difficult to reconcile with the constitutional implications and which might involve being "a bind to one's family." That she was a noticeably happier woman now than she had been for many years previously was borne out by almost every picture taken of her during the year. Slimmer, brighter, more talkative and radiant with smiles, she has carried out her duties with verve and consistency, broken only by a mild bout of influenza in January and a stomach upset in July. Even with a heavy cold in April she was still on call, sneezing her way through the Sovereign's Parade at Sandhurst on Maundy Thursday. She paid three official visits overseas. In September she went to Swaziland to represent the Queen at the Diamond Jubilee celebrations of the world's oldest monarch, King Sobhuza II. Two

A great day for Canada, but the ceremonies at which the Proclamation giving effect to the new arrangements was signed were attended by the worst possible weather. Thunder drowned the Queen's speech, but torrential rain did not deter crowds from waiting their turn to meet the Queen.

months later she was present at the formal transfer of sovereignty to Antigua, staying for two days of carnival celebrations to mark independence after three hundred years as a British colony. She witnessed a superb firework display, and was guest of honour at a luncheon party given by the Governor-General Sir Wilfred Jacobs, and held at Clarence House, the Georgian mansion where she and Lord Snowdon spent part of their honeymoon in May 1960. Finally, in February, she opened an art exhibition in Houston, Texas.

It seemed to be a year in which Princess Margaret reacquired the ability to take everything very much in her stride, though as time passed the test increased. She is usually the prime target of the sharp edge of Willie Hamilton's tongue when the Civil List increases are announced and in March he was at his most abusive. Speaking at the House of Commons to a meeting of two hundred nurses and Health Service workers who were campaigning for higher pay, he denounced her as a "useless, middle-aged floozie," pointing out that even a staff nurse's pay, if increased by the Government's offer of a

Togetherness. In contrast to the formality of the official reception two days earlier, the Queen and Prince Philip said their fond farewells to each other as they left Canada for separate destinations on 18th April. The Queen made for home, the Duke for the United States.

96

6.4% rise, would not equal the year's increase in Princess Margaret's Civil List payment, and saying that "one nurse is worth a hundred Princess Margarets." The Royal College of Nursing dissociated itself from this tirade, saying that "we would not want to be party to that sort of criticism," while Tom Benyon, the Secretary of the Tory Health and Social Services Committee, called Mr Hamilton's remarks "beneath contempt."

Last holiday before childbirth, for the Princess of Wales. She and Prince Charles visited the Scilly Isles and stayed at the Prince's cottage *Tamarisk* on St Mary's. The town of St Mary's greeted them on 20th April so effusively that a walkabout of 100 yards took nearly half an hour.

May brought a couple of less fundamental controversies. Her visit to an £11 million medical products factory in Plymouth was marred by her refusal to wear a sterile cap on her head when she toured a "clean area" where blood sample tubes were stored. A check after her visit revealed that no contamination had in fact occurred but the possibility of the loss of thousands of pounds worth of stock prompted questions as to why the Princess had refused to cover her head. Some thought she did not want to spoil her hair but the managing director said, "I would not say it was vanity. She just

ignored our request." The company's vice-chairman added, "We haven't too much experience in ordering princesses about so we took a spot decision not to press the point."

Another point was pressed more forcefully later that month when the students of Keele University decided not to invite her to their annual Christmas Ball. This now perennial problem began some four years ago when some students objected to the heavy police presence and security checks which preceded and accompanied her regular visits to the University, and in fact, although she has attended annual degree conferment ceremonies at the official invitation of its Vice-Chancellor, she has been banned from three of the last four Christmas Balls.

On the second day of their holiday the island of Tresco was sealed off so that the Prince and Princess could enjoy a private tour. They sailed from St Mary's in a locally-owned craft. The Princess, despite her cheerful wave, came back feeling a little sea-sick.

Princess Margaret paid her annual visit to the Chelsea Flower Show in May, along with other members of the Royal Family. Coincidentally, her former companion Roddy Llewellyn was also there and, in the most amicable manner, took her on a guided tour of some of the exhibits. This quite accidental encounter laid to rest any lingering rumours about a strained relationship between the two, for which the Princess will have been as grateful as she was the previous month when the last of the rumours about her most recent escort also faded.

He was 55-year-old Norman Lonsdale, a former banker, currently in the publishing trade, and a widower since 1979. His early friendship with Princess Margaret in the days of the Princess Margaret "set" blossomed again after the death of his wife, and he

was the Princess' guest in November 1981 when she spent a short holiday at "Les Jolies Eaux," her house on the island of Mustique. A budding romance was the inevitable Press story which accompanied several pictures of them both at a masked ball at the Dorchester Hotel later that month. Mr Lonsdale was again with the Princess on Mustique for a short part of her winter holiday there in February, when other guests included Colin Tennant, Lord and Lady Buckhurst and Viscount Wimborne.

When, in April, she was seen during an engagement in Glasgow wearing an unfamiliar ring on the third finger of her left hand, the rumours began to fly. Mr Lonsdale, in an effort to be as truthful and

yet as discreet as possible, produced a denial which, when suitably doctored by the Press, left everything wide open. He agreed that he and the Princess had much in common – the theatre, ballet, more than their fair share of problems – and that they got on well with each other and "laugh a lot." But he denied that he had ever given her a ring. Two days later Princess Margaret appeared in public with no

Lady Helen Windsor came of age on 28th May and Lord Snowdon took some superb portraits (opposite) to celebrate. On the same day her mother named the new RNLI lifeboat "The Duchess of Kent" at Westminster (below and bottom pictures), and Prince Charles continued his interest in the Mary Rose by taking his ninth dive (right). He also visited Cambria School Carmarthen (below right) two days later. His cousin, Viscount Linley began his final term at the John Makepeace School of Woodcraft near Beaminster, where the pictures below and opposite were taken in June.

fewer than three rings on her left hand, tantalisingly allowing the Press the briefest glimpse, and this snippet of good-humoured mischief was sufficient to put most people off the scent. But *The Sun* ran a large article headed "Happiness at Last," and perpetuated the speculation with the news that Princess Margaret would announce her engagement to Mr Lonsdale "in the next six months." The story was pooh-poohed by none other than Mr Dempster, which gave that uneasy feeling that this was just about where we came in.

The two children of Princess Margaret and Lord Snowdon,

Prince Charles was back in Wales again on 30th April to accept the Freedom of Carmarthen on behalf of the Welsh Guards in a colourful ceremony. Afterwards he changed his uniform for a walkabout in the town (below right).

having both come of age, are now beginning to make their own way in life and in the course of the year we learned a little more about how they are setting about doing so. Twenty-year-old Viscount Linley's two passions – cars and woodworking – were given full rein in a busy year. In 1981 he bought a 1966 MGB sports car and spent most of the following twelve months stripping it down and fitting a reconditioned engine. He became a member of the MG Owner's Club and in February 1982 was invited to open its new headquarters at Swavesey, in Cambridgeshire. As this was effectively his first public

appearance, and the occasion of his first public, if short, speech, there was a huge turnout of Press and public. The Club's assistant secretary said that "Viscount Linley seemed quite taken aback but coped very well." The Viscount however, assured the Press that "I shall not be doing this on a regular basis."

This was a remark typical of a young man who is fairly shy and

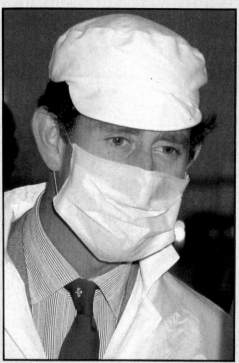

who clearly does not envy the fate of his senior cousins, whose destiny lies in the glare of publicity. In July he graduated from the John Makepeace School of Woodcraft after a two-year course which has fitted him for a career in designing, making and marketing products in wood. He left with the best possible credentials: in addition to producing some original and high quality work, much of which has been exhibited at successive Royal Shows at Stoneleigh, he has designed a useful magnet-operated hinge, which he modestly says "may be of use to industry," and has made a four-fold screen in stained wood which was snapped up by Fox Linton Associates for their exhibition in Chelsea. "It's an extremely nice piece of work," said one of the exhibition organisers. "Its strong diagonals in bright yellow, red and purple suit the modern nature of our designs." Praise too from John Makepeace himself who said that "anyone who is as determined as he is must have a promising future."

His future lies in a converted bakery in Dorking on which he and three other graduates of the school have taken a lease, and which will serve as workshops and showrooms for their products. For Viscount Linley it will be the first step towards the main Makepeace goal – independence: "I will be supporting myself," he says. Financially perhaps. Morally he will have the support of his parents: Princess Margaret has some of his pieces at Kensington Palace, and Lord Snowdon is full of encouragement: "His standard of craftsmanship is very high and his work very exciting. I think it's terribly good if someone at the age of twenty starts up on his own

Early in May, Prince Charles' visit to Brynmawr included an inspection of a computer products factory (opposite, top left) and a tour of British Steel workshops (opposite, top right). Status Quo were disappointed that he didn't wear his jeans at their concert on 14th May (opposite, centre right). Meanwhile the Queen enjoyed a two-day visit on 4th and 5th May to Liverpool (right) and Manchester (remaining pictures).

even in a small way."

Lord Snowdon was equally proud of his daughter, Lady Sarah Armstrong-Jones when, during her penultimate term at Bedales – the school which Viscount Linley had attended before joining the John Makepeace School – she won a place at the Camberwell School of Art. The news came through on Lord Snowdon's 52nd birthday

and he confessed himself "very proud. It's a very exciting start for the future." Lady Sarah's very grown-up and competent performance as the Princess of Wales' chief bridesmaid in July 1981 had been emphasised by some excellent photographic studies of her taken by her father and published in December. They provided an almost plausible excuse for the romantic speculation which followed her

The Queen missed Badminton, but saw the Windsor Horse Show in mid-May. Prince Edward turned up too, and watched Prince Philip compete in the international carriage-driving championships.

outing in March with one of Lord Mountbatten's grandsons, 20-year-old Philip Knatchbull, to see the London première of "Evil under the Sun."

# The Gloucesters

Next to the Queen Mother, Princess Alice Duchess of Gloucester is the doyenne of the Royal Family. Her eightieth birthday was celebrated on Christmas Day 1981 – not very publicly, but privately with a party at Windsor Castle at which she and that other Christmas baby, Princess Alexandra, shared the cake. The absence of any public recognition of this milestone is a shame because her work and that of her husband, the late Duke of Gloucester, in the service of the Royal Family has been as enthusiastic and as arduous as any, and 1982 sees her in her 47th year as one of its members.

She met her husband, Prince Henry, in the early thirties when, as a friend of her brother, he was a frequent guest at the family home – that of her parents the Duke and Duchess of Buccleuch. Prince Henry found himself under some pressure from his parents, King George V and Queen Mary, to marry, and after a few visits to Windsor, the then Lady Alice Montagu-Douglas-Scott was approved by them: "Mama thought Alice Scott very nice," the King wrote to his son. Six hundred telegrams flooded into Buckingham Palace on the announcement of their engagement in August 1935 and Lady Alice went up to Balmoral to be photographed with her in-laws – wearing her sister's dress as she did not have one suitable for the occasion. Because of the unexpected death of her father almost on the eve of their wedding, the plans for a Westminster Abbey ceremony were cancelled and the service was held quietly in the chapel at Buckingham Palace.

In a way it was indicative of the tenor of their married life – a quiet, retiring life with a minimum of grandeur and fuss. Both she and her husband were shy and they brought up their two children well out of the reach of publicity. In 1938 they bought Barnwell Manor in Northamptonshire, with its ruined Norman castle, which has remained the Gloucesters' country home ever since. (The castle

walls now conveniently enclose a tennis court.) But public duties allowed them little opportunity to relax, especially during and after the War, with the Duke as King George VI's senior male heir and, until 1944, the potential Regent for Princess Elizabeth. He and Princess Alice were constantly paying visits to all parts of the world – from Malta and Cyprus in the West to Malaya and Ceylon in the East – and between 1945 and 1947 they travelled almost 80,000 miles during the Duke's appointment as Governor General of Australia.

Princess Alice took on a greater proportion of royal

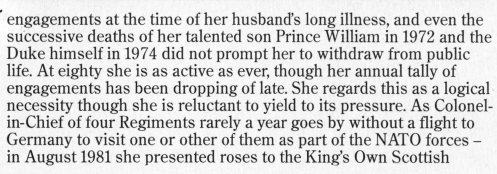

engagements at the time of her husband's long illness, and even the successive deaths of her talented son Prince William in 1972 and the Duke himself in 1974 did not prompt her to withdraw from public life. At eighty she is as active as ever, though her annual tally of engagements has been dropping of late. She regards this as a logical necessity though she is reluctant to yield to its pressure. As Colonel-in-Chief of four Regiments rarely a year goes by without a flight to Germany to visit one or other of them as part of the NATO forces – in August 1981 she presented roses to the King's Own Scottish

Borderers on Minden Day and she was back in West Germany again in May 1982. During a rare visit to Northern Ireland at the end of August 1981 she presented colours to the 5th Battalion, the Royal Irish Rangers at Ballymena, amid the usual heavy police presence.

Her, and her late husband's, long association with the Army and the many institutions which support members of our military forces made it entirely appropriate that her eightieth birthday should be marked by the presentation to her of a new rose, BLESMA Soul, by the British Limbless Ex-Serviceman's Association, of which she is Patron. In attending the ceremony of presentation at Kensington Palace on 6th January she was the first member of the Royal Family to undertake an engagement in 1982.

Of course any facts can be produced from figures, and certain mathematical exercises can be hopelessly academic and meaningless, but nevertheless it may have come as something of a surprise to discover that, according to a comparison of the number of

Prince Charles began the polo season in style. On 16th May he played for Windsor Great Park in their away match against Ham (above and right) and later that day his team won the Towry Law Cup at Windsor.

engagements carried out by each member of the Royal Family and the Civil List payments each receives, the Duke and Duchess of Gloucester represent best value for money. The discovery was revealed in a somewhat glib piece of journalism in the *Daily Express'* William Hickey column which, if nothing else, served to demonstrate that the less senior members play an important supporting role in

The Princess of Wales shared Prince Charles' afternoon polo matches more frequently than everyone expected. Her last official engagement, at Deptford on 18th May (above right and top right), came five weeks before Prince William was born, but she was still out and about at Windsor as late as 17th June (opposite page, far right).

the complex and busy system of royal participation in our national affairs. In fact, over seven hundred official engagements were carried out in 1981 by members of the Gloucester and Kent families alone.

The Duke and Duchess of Gloucester, who celebrated their tenth wedding anniversary on 8th July 1982, undertook almost two hundred of these in their quiet, unobtrusive and thoroughly uncontroversial way – indeed the only helping of notoriety either of them attracted came when the Duke was fined £38 for exceeding the speed limit near Barnwell Manor. But it was a year of foreign journeys for them as no other year had been. In September the Duke led a delegation of trade officials from the British Consultants Bureau to Rangoon, Burma for three days, doing very much what his late brother found was his forte, and in February he and his wife – forsaking the Swiss ski-slopes for once – travelled to Nepal for a three-week private holiday with a party of half a dozen friends. They were greeted by King Birendra of Nepal, a close friend of many members of the British Royal Family and of the Duke in particular who was at Eton with him, and were entertained to supper before

beginning a fortnight's trekking expedition in the Himalayan foothills – just as Prince Charles did for a much shorter period in December 1980. They arrived back home on 14th March, both looking dishevelled after their long flight, and with the Duke sporting the beginnings of a beard. Two days later he had shaved it off in time to welcome the Sultan of Oman on his arrival at Gatwick Airport for his three-day visit to Britain.

The Duke and Duchess welcomed two other royal guests from abroad in the course of the year: in mid-November Prince Albert and

A caring Duchess of Kent met handicapped children at St James's Palace on 24th May (this page) when she presented three Sunshine Coaches donated by the Variety Club of Great Britain. On the same day, the Duchess of Gloucester presented music teaching awards at Wedgwoods in Wigmore Street (opposite page, far right). Princess Margaret spent an evening at the ballet – seeing *Swan Lake* – on 25th May.

Princess Paola of the Belgians came to Britain for celebrations to mark the 150th anniversary of the founding of the Belgian royal dynasty by King Leopold, an uncle of the Duke's great-great-grandmother Queen Victoria, and later the same month Queen Margrethe II of Denmark came to the British Museum to give a lecture on the history of Rosenborg Castle, the 17th-century home and mausoleum of generations of Danish monarchs, and on its collection of royal treasures.

In April the Duke and Duchess attended a ceremony at the

Guildhall, Gloucester in which they both received the Freedom of the city from which they take their title.

# ❧ The Kents

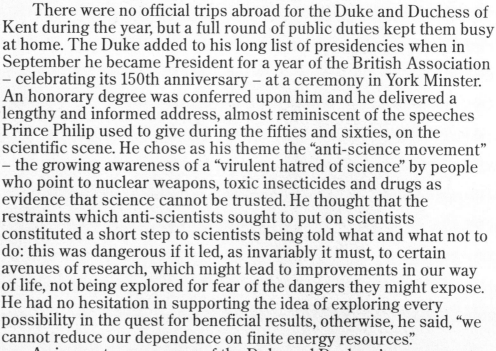

There were no official trips abroad for the Duke and Duchess of Kent during the year, but a full round of public duties kept them busy at home. The Duke added to his long list of presidencies when in September he became President for a year of the British Association – celebrating its 150th anniversary – at a ceremony in York Minster. An honorary degree was conferred upon him and he delivered a lengthy and informed address, almost reminiscent of the speeches Prince Philip used to give during the fifties and sixties, on the scientific scene. He chose as his theme the "anti-science movement" – the growing awareness of a "virulent hatred of science" by people who point to nuclear weapons, toxic insecticides and drugs as evidence that science cannot be trusted. He thought that the restraints which anti-scientists sought to put on scientists constituted a short step to scientists being told what and what not to do: this was dangerous if it led, as invariably it must, to certain avenues of research, which might lead to improvements in our way of life, not being explored for fear of the dangers they might expose. He had no hesitation in supporting the idea of exploring every possibility in the quest for beneficial results, otherwise, he said, "we cannot reduce our dependence on finite energy resources."

As in most years, many of the Duke and Duchess' engagements were linked to the fact that they are President or Patron of many different organisations. As Grand Master, the Duke attended many Masonic meetings throughout the year, as Patron of the Royal

Television Society he attended its Schoenberg Lecture in November, and as honorary President of the Geographical Society he presided at its 151st anniversary dinner. His presidency of the All England Lawn Tennis Association – a post he has held since the death of his mother Princess Marina in 1968 – took him and the Duchess to Wimbledon in July 1981 and July 1982 to watch the championships on several different days, and to present trophies after the finals. And as President of the Royal National Lifeboat Institution both he and the Duchess launched or presented lifeboats to be put into service to continue the Institution's century-old tradition of efficient and dedicated life-saving.

In that capacity the Duke and Duchess travelled to Mousehole in January to attend a service in commemoration of eight lifeboatmen from the Cornish village of Penlee who lost their lives on 19th

December 1981, when their boat *Solomon Browne* was smashed against rocks during an abortive attempt to save a ship in distress. After the service, during which the Duke read the Lesson, they both spoke privately with the widows and orphans of the dead, who were as impressed by their concern as the Duke was by the fortitude of

The Queen, as Sovereign, and Prince Charles, as Grand Master, attended another Service for the installation of Knights of the Order of the Bath at Westminster Abbey on 27th May (opposite). Two days earlier, Prince Charles accompanied Prince Philip to the annual Court and service of Trinity House in London (right).

the bereaved: "It was magnificent to meet families who have shown so much courage," he said.

Many of the Duchess' public duties reflected her personal love of music. In September she presented awards at the Leeds piano competition in which 24-year-old Ian Hobson came first, at his second attempt at this prestigious international event, and in December she attended a ceremony conferring Fellowships of the Royal Northern College of Music, of which she is President, in Manchester. The Duchess maintained her long association with the

Bach Choir, attending weekly rehearsals and singing with them in most of their year's programme of concerts. In February she sang at their performance of the Berlioz *Requiem,* attended by the Prince and Princess of Wales, at the Royal Albert Hall. She was, however, unable to join the Choir on their tour of Hong Kong at Easter because of the possibility – which failed to materialise – that she and the Duke would be making an official visit there around the same time. In events it made little difference because at the end of March the Duchess was whisked into hospital for a week for the removal of a benign obstruction in her gall bladder duct – the latest of a series of indispositions of various kinds since her miscarriage in 1977. She was out again shortly before Easter – just in time, ironically, to open a new medical surgery in Norfolk.

It is now over twenty years since the Duke and Duchess were married – at York Minster on 8th June 1961 – and although their twentieth wedding anniversary passed off almost unnoticed, the public spotlight fell on two of their growing family of three children.

A forty-minute meeting between the Pope and the Queen at Buckingham Palace caused consternation for some, but made history for all, on 28th May.

After last year's academic successes of their eldest son, George, Earl of St Andrews, it was very much Lady Helen Windsor's year as, on 28th April, she reached her eighteenth birthday. It was marked, officially, in an almost flamboyant manner, by the issue of three portrait photographs of her, taken by Lord Snowdon, all of which provided conclusive evidence that she is no longer the adolescent schoolgirl but a mature and attractive young lady giving every promise that she will be as sophisticated, in dress and manner, as her mother. At the time the photographs were taken, she was about to

begin her last term at Gordonstoun School, like her cousin Prince Edward, where she took her 'A' levels in English, Art and the History of Art. Meanwhile her younger brother Lord Nicholas Windsor, who had his eleventh birthday just four days before he acted as page to the Princess of Wales at her wedding, spent his penultimate year at his prep school, Sussex House, in Chelsea.

The entire family left Britain after Christmas for a fortnight's skiing holiday at the French ski resort of Meribel. The holiday was to some extent clouded by the news that Heather Goodchild, who was nanny to the Kents' children and who accompanied them to Meribel, had become involved in a marital dispute and had been accused of "stealing" Sergeant Arthur Povey, a cook at St James's Palace. The accusation came from Sergeant Povey's wife and was denied by none other than the Duke himself in a rare interview, bearing as it did on personal matters relating to his staff. He

dismissed Mrs Povey's claim as "total fabrication. As I understand the situation the marriage was over long before Heather met Sergeant Povey. The Duchess and I are very fond of Heather and we are standing by her, naturally, and we totally support her."

As it happened Miss Goodchild left the Kents' service shortly afterwards though for reasons unconnected with the affair, which provided the only hint of any controversy in the course of the year as a whole. If the family needed any compensating bouquets, one came in mid-May when, quite out of the blue, the Duchess was selected as one of the seven most sophisticated women in Britain. The choice was made by the Ronald Joyce organisation, which manufactures evening dresses, on the basis of something more than the ability to dress well. Its chairman, Ronald Phillips, explained that the Duchess "is the ultimate in English chic and always looks highly sophisticated – a fine example for many women to follow." As she approaches, incredibly, her fiftieth birthday on 22nd February 1983, she will, in her modest way, be more than gratified by this unsolicited compliment to one of the most popular members of the Royal Family.

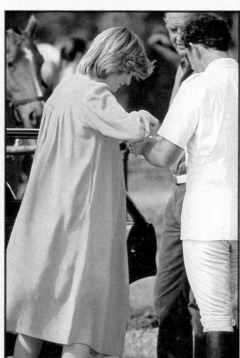

# Prince Michael

It would be churlish and over-technical to exclude Prince and Princess Michael of Kent in an account of the year's activities within the Royal Family. Prince Michael gave up his claim to the Throne on his marriage in 1978, and the functions which he and his wife attend are neither funded from the Civil List nor mentioned in the official Court Circular. But they remain members of the Royal Family

Fun for all. Prince Charles joined enthusiastic youngsters and organisers at the Capital Radio Venture Day at Battersea Park on 6th June. Higher class fun surrounded the Derby at Epsom on 2nd June: the Royal Family, including Prince and Princess Michael (opposite, top right), were out in force.

nevertheless and the point was emphasised in September when the Queen sent them to Belize to attend the independence celebrations. The visit took place immediately after the Prince and Princess had returned from a three day private trip to Czechoslovakia – the Princess was born there – and at the end of a six week Summer break during which Prince Michael had grown a beard for the second time. It was not there when he accompanied his wife in the Prince of Wales' wedding procession at the end of July, but he sported a luxuriant growth by September as the official portraits released to coincide with their Belize visit proved. For pedantic guardians of protocol the beard raised technical difficulties, for it was pointed out that regulations would be contravened if it was to be worn with military uniform. The Prince quit the Army the previous Spring with the rank of Major in The Royal Hussars but had obtained the Queen's consent to continue to wear uniform. The difficulty was that the only officer permitted to wear a beard with the uniform, except for health reasons, was a regimental pioneer sergeant. However, it seemed that Prince Michael had probably had an extra word with the Queen, since it was confirmed that "considerable efforts" had been made to ensure that military etiquette was not offended. Beard, plus uniform, were after all permitted.

Polo at Windsor again – on 5th June – and the Queen was there to present her Cup. The Princess of Wales cheered her husband's team on, but they had to be content with runners-up medals.

The celebrations in Belize were very nearly ruined by the weather – the least of the new state's worries in view of neighbouring Guatemala's claims on it – because, just an hour before the midnight ceremony when the flags were due to be lowered and raised and the documents of independence handed over, a violent thunderstorm brought torrential rain and sent Prince and Princess Michael, and their one thousand guests, scurrying for shelter. Mercifully the rain stopped just in time for the official ceremonies to take place as planned and the day was saved.

Prince Michael paid a three-day official visit to Jordan the following March, but generally the engagements which he and Princess Michael undertook during the year reflected their own personal interests rather than the obligations to which other members of the Royal Family commit themselves. For instance, the

Prince is a keen enthusiast of bobsleighing, despite the accident in 1970 in which he was almost killed, and has for some time been President of the British Bobsleigh Association. As such he opened a training run in Chertsey in September, and visited St Moritz in January to see the British teams at work competing in the world championships. He is also interested in sailing and took his wife to Cowes in March where she named the *Victory,* the new British challenger for the America's Cup, and where she delighted onlookers by kicking off her shoes and jumping from the quayside to the yacht in her stockinged feet in order to inspect her. Both the Prince and Princess enjoy equestrian events: Prince Michael hunted regularly with the Quorn during the year, Princess Michael attended the Beaufort point-to-point at Didmarton in Gloucestershire in March, and both attended Badminton Horse Trials in April and Epsom in June.

At the other extreme of their combined interests is their penchant for the arts. Like her talented mother-in-law, Princess Marina, Princess Michael paints, though "very badly" she admits, "in water colours," preferring to paint still life and flowers: "I don't paint as well as Princess Marina did and feel I have a lot to live up to." Her ambition is to have one of her works accepted by the Society of Women Artists, whose annual exhibition she opened at the Mall Galleries in February. The cinema and theatre also have Prince

Michael's support: he visited the Cannes Film Festival in May specifically to see how the film *Moonlighting* would fare. This film, starring Jeremy Irons, was one of three official British entries this year, and Prince Michael backed it financially. Among the films and

First Presidential stay at Windsor. President Reagan and his wife Nancy arrived at Heathrow (bottom) on 7th June, and were taken to Windsor to meet the Queen (bottom right) and Prince Charles. The President inspected the thin red lines (right).

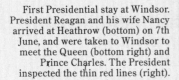

plays Prince and Princess Michael saw during the year were *The Little Foxes* in March, when they met Elizabeth Taylor – the charity première of *On Golden Pond* at the Empire Leicester Square, and the new £1½ million production of *The Pirates of Penzance* at the Savoy. Rumour had it that the Prince and Princess could even be going

into television, with Prince Michael as non-executive director of the television company AMTV and his wife as a breakfast television presenter. Even their private secretary was quoted as saying "Indeed why not? It's an intriguing suggestion."

But all is quiet on the front at present: perhaps Princess Michael is too busy finishing her book on Elizabeth of Bohemia – the Winter Queen, daughter of our own King James I and a direct ancestress of the House of Windsor.

It was during a visit to Holland to research for the book that, on 16th February, Princess Michael was taken ill with severe abdominal pains. She was rushed off to King Edward VII Hospital for Officers

in Marylebone, where two days of examination and tests amid rumours that she was pregnant or had suffered a miscarriage showed that her gall bladder was the cause of the trouble. Prince Michael was at her bedside for most of a worrying time, and even brought their two children to see their mother who "was missing them, and the doctors thought it would be a tonic for her." Lord

After the formalities of the first day, a gentle canter in Home Park put the Queen and the President where they like to be. Prince Philip and Mrs Reagan preferred a more sedate form of transport.

Frederick looked a picture in his piped jacket and knickerbockers! After an operation for the removal of her gall bladder, Princess Michael emerged from hospital "feeling fine" on 1st March, and went back to Kensington Palace to catch up on her work.

By "work" she was probably referring to her book, but it should be borne in mind that with 120 engagements to their credit in 1981 Prince and Princess Michael undertook as many as Princess Alexandra and more than Princess Margaret. It indicates that in spite of their constitutional position they are as willing as any to maintain the Royal Family's involvement in the everyday events of ordinary people, and Princess Michael's particular flair for her job provides ample evidence. "What refreshes me about Princess Michael of Kent,"

On 10th June, the Queen inspected the 300th anniversary parade of the Chelsea In-pensioners under the statue of Charles II swathed in oak leaves.

wrote Jean Rook in the *Daily Express* in October, "is her shameless love of being royal." The sentiment has been often expressed and genuinely felt. Quite apart from her spectacular wardrobe and sparkling jewellery, she has established a regal, yet pleasantly informal and natural rapport with people which has probably not been adequately acknowledged, and which may never be fully appreciated while she and Prince Michael remain, as they must, within the junior, and thus less publicised, branches of the Royal Family.

# Princess Alexandra

For Princess Alexandra, one of the least conspicuous members of the Royal Family, but one who has never lost the popularity she attracted during the early nineteen-sixties, the year has been a quiet one in which she has continued her work of assisting the many good

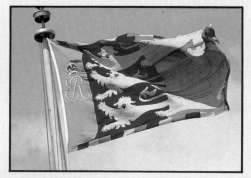

On his birthday, 10th June, Prince Philip took the Salute at Beating the Retreat on Horse Guards (opposite page, bottom left). Next day the Queen Mother returned to Portsmouth from her three-day tour of the Channel ports. *Britannia* brought her back.

causes with which she is involved. In a period which has seen the closing of the International Year of the Disabled, she seems to have paid particular attention to the underprivileged in terms of health of mind and body. As Vice-President of the Red Cross Society – she attended one of its meetings in mid-October – she went to Derbyshire at the end of October to be at a party for disabled children, given by the Society. Having attended a dinner the following March in aid of the U.K. Special Olympics for handicapped people, she opened the 1982 Games at Knowsley, on Merseyside on 6th July.

Mental health also commands the Princess' sympathies: she is Patron of the Mental Health Foundation and attended not only its Annual General Meeting in November, but also a fashion show at the Japanese Embassy Residence in January (the proceeds of which went to the Foundation), the Memorial Service for Lord Butler of

Saffron Walden in April – he was a benefactor of the Foundation from its earliest days – and a special preview of the television film *Someone to Talk to,* produced in July by Thames Television in association with the Foundation.

In the more general field of health, Princess Alexandra's connections seem endless and many of them won her attention during the year. In October she attended a service in Brighton to commemorate the centenary of the Royal Alexandra Hospital for Sick Children of which, like her founding great-grandmother Queen

The Queen endured the wettest Trooping ever with tolerance, and even cheerfulness, on 12th June. There was no repetition of the previous year's drama.

Alexandra, she is Patron. Still on the theme of children, she went to Carshalton in April to open the Rainbow Centre, a new child development unit of the Queen Mary Hospital for Children. The opening in September of the Wolfson Building, Moorfield Hospital's new international centre for eye health in London, was complemented by her attendance as Patron at the 125th anniversary celebrations of the London Association of the Blind the following July. She attended a buffet lunch for delegates attending the National Pain Relief Conference in October, and a concert in aid of the

National Kidney Fund, of which, again, she is Patron, in June. More generally, another concert she attended in February assisted the Council for Music in Hospitals, and as Governor of the King Edward VII Hospital for Officers – where both her sisters-in-law had been treated for gall-bladder complaints earlier in the year – she took part in its Annual General Meeting in June.

Princess Alexandra maintained her honorary connections with the Services and their offshoots by taking the Salute at the Beating the Retreat ceremony in June, and by paying visits to the 2nd Battalion Light Infantry at their camp at Weeton, Lancashire in November and to the Royal Yeomanry at Warcop Camp, Cumbria the previous September – the month she also visited the Redhill Headquarters of the Girls Venture Corps.

In a family which is slowly acquiring a more appreciative leaning towards the arts, Princess Alexandra has been among the front-runners, and an impressive tally of her engagements this year demonstrated her continuing interest, from music to archaeology. She attended two concerts to celebrate famous composers' birthdays – Malcolm Williamson's 50th in October, and Sir William Walton's 80th the following March – and a thanksgiving concert in aid of the Janet Craxton Memorial Trust in April. As Vice-Patron of the Royal Over-Seas League she attended both the semi-finals in April, and the finals in June, of its 30th annual Music Festival. A keen theatre-goer, the Princess is Patron of the Central School of Speech and Drama, and attended a performance to celebrate its 75th anniversary in October. She had already seen *Cavalcade* at Farnham Rep. earlier that month and in May she saw the new version of *The Pirates of Penzance* at Drury Lane. In the visual arts she opened one of *Maritime England's* many exhibitions of 1982 – entitled *The Art of the Van der Veldes* – at Greenwich in June, attended a special preview of the Fine Arts and Antiques Fair, loaned some of her jewellery to the highly successful Burlington House Fair at the Royal Academy of Arts, and visited the exhibition *Excavating Egypt* at the British Museum in February.

The farming community received Princess Alexandra's patronage in June and July, when she visited no fewer than three agricultural shows in five weeks – the Bath and West at Shepton Mallet, the Royal Norfolk at Norwich and the Kent County Show at Detling near Maidstone. She paid no less attention to her position as Chancellor of the University of Lancaster, presiding at two degree conferment ceremonies in October and another six during a three-day visit to Lancashire in July. Lancaster University held no charms, however, for her son James who, having passed three 'A' levels – in History, Politics and the History of Art – at the age of seventeen in 1981, left Eton in order to improve on his grades before, he hopes, going to Oxford in October 1982. His father, the Hon. Angus Ogilvy, was at Trinity College Oxford in the late 1940's and James is obviously keen to follow in his footsteps. Like other members of the Kent families he has a pronounced artistic streak: he is a good pianist, keen on architecture, and an accomplished photographer.

Princess Alexandra's only official foreign visit abroad was to Washington in May, where she opened *Lutyens 82: A British Embassy Showcase.* The engagement was a hastily-arranged one, concocted out of circumstances of some chaos left in the wake of the Falklands dispute. Lord Carrington was originally due to open the exhibition as Foreign Secretary, but his resignation at the beginning of April made it necessary for other arrangements to be made. As it happened, Princess Alexandra had been due to make a fortnight's official and semi-official visit to Peru from 29th April to 12th May, which itself was postponed a week before it was scheduled to begin, when the dispute over the Falklands had deteriorated into undeclared war. To fill the gap in the Princess' diary she was engaged to go to Washington in place of Lord Carrington.

## Conclusion

In fact the Falklands war became the spark for a great deal of royal activity after April and put into jeopardy one event that, above all others, had been occupying people's minds constantly since the beginning of 1982. A year earlier it had been announced that the Pope would pay a pastoral visit to Britain in April and May 1982, and by the end of 1981 arrangements for his journeyings to London, Cardiff, Glasgow, Manchester, Coventry, Canterbury and so on were well in hand. It had been agreed that he would speak with the Queen – a

returned compliment following her audience with him in 1980 – at a 40-minute meeting at Buckingham Palace on 28th May. It was a meeting that all sorts of people were looking forward to for all sorts of reasons, but the fact that it would constitute the first encounter between a Pontiff and a British sovereign on British soil since the breach with Rome in the 1530's made it an event of great historical significance. Ultra-Protestants saw the visit as a pernicious development in the undesirable process, for them, of unity between the Anglican Church and the Church of Rome, and campaigned long, hard and relatively peaceably for its cancellation. But the Falklands crisis nearly achieved what they were unable to accomplish by their own efforts. By the end of April Britain was deep into conflict with Argentina and the Holy Father let it be known that a mission to a

country in the throes of war would be impossible. Nuncios and cardinals flew in constant streams between London and Rome in an effort to persuade the Pope to adhere to his original plans and eventually the political content of the tour was so effectively neutralised that, with the added promise of a subsequent Papal visit to Argentina, the British tour went ahead. Accordingly the Queen became the first Sovereign to entertain a Pope at Buckingham Palace – even for only forty minutes.

Of course, Prince Andrew's involvement in the war brought its

A welcome return home was followed by the traditional balcony appearance. Amazingly, the crowds stayed in the rain to cheer as the Queen and her family – including, again, the Princess of Wales, only nine days from motherhood – made their customary acknowledgement of the RAF's fly-past.

worries and fears directly home to the Queen and for once she and her family were no mere consolers of other people's griefs and uncertainties. Late in May she allowed herself to show genuine sorrow as she spoke, during the opening of the Keilder Dam in Northumberland, of those who had just lost their lives in the sinking of *HMS Coventry,* and she had been reminded of the dangers earlier in the month when one of the cast of *Coronation Street,* whose new set she was inspecting in Manchester, assured her of their concern for the welfare of Prince Andrew. By early June the tide had begun to

On a cool day, the Garter Ceremony at Windsor was much like any other year's proceedings. The Duke of Edinburgh was absent, attending the funeral of the King of Saudi Arabia, so Prince Charles, who escorted the Queen Mother in the walking procession to St George's Chapel (below right and opposite), accompanied the Queen on the way back (below).

swing demonstrably in Britain's favour and the Queen's mood changed quite dramatically by the time President Reagan paid his official visit to Windsor Castle. In a speech following a State Banquet at Windsor Castle she positively blasted the Argentinians for the "naked aggression" which had imposed the war upon Britain. They were confident words, based on the virtual certainty that the Task Force, with its enormous resources for a mobile, sea-based operation, was well on its way to ultimate victory.

Four days of Royal Ascot from 15th to 18th June brought the Royal Family out in some of their brightest clothes. Even Prince Philip seemed to be enjoying himself (opposite page, top).

Victory, when it came, spelt out more duties for the Royal Family, increasing the already heavy workload which normally precedes the holiday months of August and September. By the beginning of July some of the ships were on their way home: in June the *Queen Elizabeth 2* had, greeted by the Queen Mother *en route,* sailed into Southampton with survivors of three sinkings; now a succession of homecomings, each glorified by the presence of royalty, captured the popular imagination. Some of those homecomings were less than joyful, involving as they did men who had been injured on active service, and the Royal Family's attentions were directed to them as

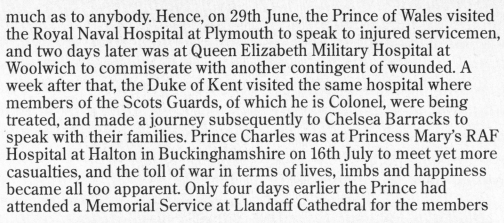

much as to anybody. Hence, on 29th June, the Prince of Wales visited the Royal Naval Hospital at Plymouth to speak to injured servicemen, and two days later was at Queen Elizabeth Military Hospital at Woolwich to commiserate with another contingent of wounded. A week after that, the Duke of Kent visited the same hospital where members of the Scots Guards, of which he is Colonel, were being treated, and made a journey subsequently to Chelsea Barracks to speak with their families. Prince Charles was at Princess Mary's RAF Hospital at Halton in Buckinghamshire on 16th July to meet yet more casualties, and the toll of war in terms of lives, limbs and happiness became all too apparent. Only four days earlier the Prince had attended a Memorial Service at Llandaff Cathedral for the members

of the Welsh Guards who had perished during the war.

Meanwhile, the luckier members of the Forces were now streaming into the country. Prince Charles went to RAF Brize Norton twice; on 6th July to welcome home members of the Paratroop Regiment, and on the 29th – his first wedding anniversary – to greet the Welsh Guards on their return. Prince Philip, too, was at Plymouth on 13th July and at Poole on 28th and 29th – on both occasions to visit the Royal Marines who had played a vital and experienced part in the successful recapture of the Islands. But the real essence – a victorious return celebrated by the people and graced by royalty –

The Queen presented prizes at Windsor Great Park on 17th June, after one of a series of evening polo matches there, arranged as a follow-up to the afternoon racing at Ascot.

was encapsulated in three major events in just over two busy weeks in July. On the 11th Prince Charles flew his Wessex helicopter onto *HMS Canberra* just two hours before she was due to berth at Southampton carrying over two thousand jubilant troops, most of them unscathed but glad to be back from an experience they would never want to repeat. A week later, the Prince attended a massive variety performance at the London Coliseum at which over three hundred entertainers gave their services free in aid of the South Atlantic Fund which had been set up a few weeks earlier under his patronage. And on 26th July the entire adult complement of the Royal Family, except Princess Margaret who was holidaying in Italy, attended a moving and dignified service of thanksgiving and commemoration in St Paul's Cathedral, in honour of the peace, those on both sides of the conflict who fell, and those who provided outstanding examples of leadership, dedication and courage.

The public anticipation of this service was heightened partly by the controversy which surrounded it – there were rumours that the Church and the Government could not agree on the balance of patriotism and meditation – and partly by the first public appearance of the Princess of Wales since the birth of her baby in June. That event of course was the highlight of the year, the ephemeral royal occurrence which made everyone forget the difficulties of the past, crowned the present with success, and filled the future with hope. Any day would have been thought a fitting day for his birth, but 21st June was the longest day of the year and the first day of what already seemed to be a glorious summer. The Princess had gone into hospital at five in the morning, the latest in a long line of royal mothers to use an everyday hospital – even one like St Mary's Paddington whose Lindo Wing rooms cost £128 a day – for their confinements, and scotching all the rumours about continuing the tradition of having a future king born within the confines of a royal home. Prince Charles went with her, and stayed with her, thus

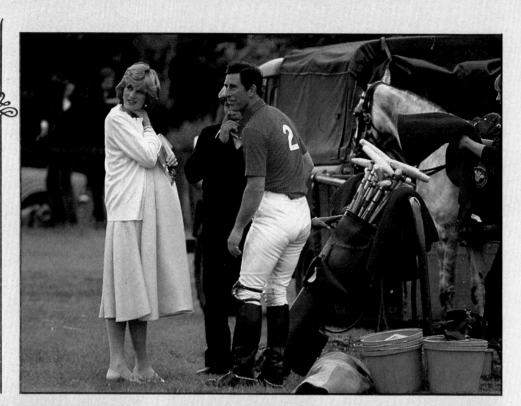

Prince Charles savoured his victory with some sugar lumps for his ponies and an affectionate hug for his wife. She had said before that she enjoyed polo really, and now looked as if she did.

becoming the first royal father since the Prince Consort to see his son and heir born. "It was a bit of a shock to my system," he said afterwards, as he emerged looking none the worse for wear after his wife's sixteen-hour labour, and with a fierce lipstick mark on his cheek which proved that, even as a happily married man safely out of the reach of the thousands of would-be Princesses of Wales who only two years before jostled their way through crowds to kiss him, he can still slay the women. The Queen and Prince Philip had spent most of the day with the Royal Air Force Regiment at RAF Wittering

in Cambridgeshire, but the Queen at least was back in Buckingham Palace long before the good news was announced to her by telephone. The precise time of the birth – 9.03 pm – was important only to the officials who had to complete the pre-typed bulletin for display on the Palace gates, and to the astrologers who died a

thousand deaths while the event hovered between the influences of Gemini and Cancer. For the other 99.9% of Britain's population and for countless millions the world over, it was enough that the birth, though long drawn-out as first births often are, was straightforward and safely accomplished. Britain, like Prince Charles, went to bed that night feeling a sense of vicarious achievement.

In the faintly hysterical circumstances which brought Britain a new heir shortly after victory in the South Atlantic and possible

victory in the World Cup – the other main preoccupations of a country on the verge of the silly season – it was not surprising that suggestions for the names of the new Prince should have included Stanley, after the capital of the Falklands, and Ron, after the

The Queen with her forces: visiting the Royal Air Force Regiment at Wittering on 21st June (above); and with the Police at Chichester a week later (top left and opposite page, right).

manager of the England football team. Happily, and not surprisingly, the Prince and Princess chose some fairly uncontroversial family names out of the dozens which must have suggested themselves. The first, William, was selected because they liked it and to avoid any confusion with other members of the family – there was already for instance a George, a James, a Philip, an Edward and, of course, a Charles. Arthur, Philip and Louis, all of which, save possibly Arthur, had been highly tipped, were his supplementary names and the entire string formed the now traditional quartet of names given to sons and daughters of the Sovereign. To those looking far into the future, King William V had a strange ring to it but a period of potentially fifty years is a long time in which to accustom oneself to anything.

But it was also time to look back. Almost every major royal birth

Prince's début. After visits on 22nd June by the Queen and Earl Spencer (pictures below) the Prince and Princess of Wales left the Lindo Wing of St Mary's Hospital Paddington with the infant Prince William. He was born at 9.03 pm the previous day and Prince Charles appeared two hours later, in jubilant mood (right).

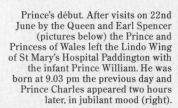

since Queen Victoria's time has had that unique distinction of completing the "four generations" phenomenon which the future King Edward VIII's birth in 1894 so popularised. Prince Charles, with what he freely admits to as an "overdeveloped sense of history," created a *coup de théâtre* out of that same phenomenon by fixing 4th August – the 82nd birthday of Queen Elizabeth the Queen Mother –

as christening day for her great-grandson and the ultimate successor to her late husband King George VI. A small army of friends and relatives gathered at Buckingham Palace that morning and watched as, in the palatial privacy of the Music Room, the Archbishop of Canterbury poured water from the River Jordan over the young Prince's forehead, and received him into the Christian faith. Among those present were the six godparents, representing a wider

Lord Snowdon's 21st birthday portrait of the Princess of Wales (below) was released on 1st July. Four weeks later, on her first wedding anniversary, came these pictures which delighted the world.

spectrum of life than was once the case: a Princess, Alexandra; an ex-King, Constantine of Greece; the Duchess of Westminster, Lord Romsey, Lady Susan Hussey and the writer Laurens van der Post. By all accounts young Prince William behaved well but the subsequent photographic session proved less tolerable to him and the lady who

The return of the *Hermes* in July (opposite) provided the opportunity to celebrate the South Atlantic victory. The service of thanksgiving and commemoration at St Paul's, attended by nearly the whole Royal Family at the end of the month, played down the obsessive patriotism.

offered her cheek for the first public kiss on Buckingham Palace's balcony now offered a finger as a temporary substitute for the next feed.

Amid the laughter and transparent happiness of the occasion the Queen above all must have felt that this secure and successful outcome of almost a year's preoccupation provided an appropriate celebration of this her thirtieth year as Britain's sovereign. Certain it is that the memory of that early August day will abide far longer than the tumultuous days of the previous month, when she must have wondered what she had done to deserve it all. A more leisurely look back over the entire twelve months manifests a quite different interpretation of the Royal Year – one which for the family as a whole was busy, eventful, dedicated and successful, and which puts July 1982 into perspective as just one of those months in which life became a little too hectic.

Prince William's christening. Four generations at Buckingham Palace on 4th August – the Queen Mother's 82nd birthday. The lace christening robe is 142-years old.

First English edition published by Colour Library International Ltd.
© 1982 Illustrations: Keystone Press Agency, London and Camera Press, London.
© 1982 Text: Colour Library International Limited, Guildford, Surrey, England
   99 Park Avenue, New York, N.Y. 10016, U.S.A.
This edition is published by Crescent Books.
Distributed by Crown Publishers, Inc.
h g f e d c b a
Colour separations by LLOVET, Barcelona, Spain.
Display and text filmsetting by ACESETTERS LTD., Richmond, Surrey, England.
Printed and bound in Barcelona, Spain by RIEUSSET and EUROBINDER.

Library of Congress Catalog Card No. 82-70295
CRESCENT BOOKS 1982

D.L.B.: 36298-82